Unbelievable Crimes Volume Four

Unbelievable Crimes, Volume 4

Daniela Airlie

GW00567889

Published by Daniela Airlie, 2023.

UNBELIEVABLE CRIMES VOLUME FOUR

First edition. July 12, 2023.

Written by Daniela Airlie.

Table of Contents

Unbelievable Crimes Volume Four 1

Introduction 3

The Mocking Murderer 7

A Longing To Kill 19

The Devil's Daughter 31

A True Horror Script 41

Revenge Gone Too Far 51

A World Of Cruelty 63

Injustice 73

A Thrill Killing 79

Evil Infatuation 93

Murder For Motherhood 103

Final Thoughts 111

Introduction

Welcome to the fourth installment of *Unbelievable Crimes*. This series is an ongoing journey through the darkest depths of our existence, uncovering stories kept out of sight from even the most knowledgeable true crime follower. For those new to this series, the Unbelievable Crimes anthologies cover disturbing cases and little-heard true crime stories, exposing the culprits and, in some small way, ensuring victims' voices aren't blotted out of the annals of true crime history.

In this installment, I'll cover ten crimes that seemed to evade public knowledge when they took place, for the most part, at least. This begs the question, why do some crimes etch themselves into our minds forever, while others are destined to be forgotten without so much as a small section in the local newspaper? The crimes I cover throughout this book are no less shocking or deplorable than Ted Bundy's crimes. Yet his name became seared into almost everybody's vocabulary, while the equally unbelievable and tragic crimes of plenty of other murderous monsters barely get a mention on the news. More importantly, this means the victims don't get a mention, causing their tales to be buried deep in the true crime archives. *Why?*

I think it's a difficult question to answer because it's multifaceted. Ted Bundy, Jeffery Dahmer, and Jack The Ripper dominate the true crime landscape. These are household names even for those who\ don't pay much heed to true crime cases. I came to the conclusion that crimes less heard of are forgotten about due to unfortunate timing - perhaps other, "bigger" news stories took precedence at that time - and geography plays a big part in how much a crime story is covered, too.

Marginalized communities that suffer a crime may find their story gets buried underneath others. Human bias and judgment may also play a part in if - and how - a story is told. For example, the amount of headlines that read like "drug-addicted prostitute dies" instead of "mother-of-two brutally murdered" is mind-boggling. The first headline could cause people to turn the page out of judgment, or perhaps worse, read the news story and blame the victim. The latter, more accurate title, evokes emotion and addresses a tragic murder, capturing the reader's desire to understand what happened.

We trust the media to deliver us news from faraway places, as well as our local news stories, but it's up to them to pick and choose which ones are worthy of their screen time. This is why I cover tales from various locations, varying communities, and social classes, so we are exposed to terrible acts we'd not be aware of otherwise.

There are plenty of books on notorious criminals and their vile acts. There are even more documentaries and TV series covering them. I'm avoiding those cases as best I can. I agree the victims of those crimes haven't had their stories told as much as they ought to have, but their killer's actions are still reviled and condemned by the masses. That's not necessarily the case for the crimes I'm covering. Overlooked stories deserve - demand, even - to be heard.

As always, Volume Four will shine a light to expose crimes you've not yet heard of. And, as I always repeat, please know this book details suffering and descriptions of real crimes - bear this in mind if you feel this topic is too heavy for you. With that said, let's begin.

The Mocking Murderer

Sometimes, in criminal cases, you have a special breed of criminal: those who feel so untouchable that they goad the police or their victims. In some cases, this arrogance ends up putting the criminal behind bars. That was the case for the Bind, Torture, Kill murderer years ago (a name he gave himself, one the press abbreviated to "*BTK*"). Giving yourself your serial killer name is conceited enough, but BTK, aka Dennis Rader, went much further than that.

The evil man took the lives of 10 people between the mid-70s and early 90s in truly sadistic and revolting ways. By 2004, Rader hadn't murdered anyone in 13 years. His crimes were still being investigated, although the case was beyond cold at this point. The hopes of finding the killer were slim, but it didn't stop the police from trying. The case would have likely stayed ice cold if the egotistical killer hadn't felt the urge to rear his head and taunt the police and media for their inability to capture him.

To mark the thirteenth year of the (still unknown) killer and his heinous crimes, the stories of BTK's victims began to reappear on TV and in newspapers. This sudden jolt of renewed interest in the killings ignited Rader's lust to return to the spotlight as his murderous alter ego, BTK.

He began sending messages to the police and the media outlets reporting his crimes from years prior. In particular, he was corresponding with Detective Ken Landwehr. In his communications, Rader sent photos of his crime scenes and even sent a photocopy of one of his victim's driving licenses. He would sign his letters off as "Bill Thomas Killman," a name it seems he perhaps thought was an incredibly clever play on words. He warned he was going to kill again and already had a victim in mind; in fact, he was actively stalking them. Macabrely, Rader would also leave taunting packages for the police, which would have a doll inside that was bound at the hands and feet like his victims were.

After almost a year of back and forth with Ken Landwehr, Rader asked the detective if he could send him a floppy disk without incriminating himself by doing so. Ken replied that there was no way the police would be able to trace the particular computer used when opening the data from the floppy disk. This was a lie.

A few weeks passed, and Ken got a package as expected. Inside was the floppy disk. It didn't take long for the disk to be traced right back to Dennis Lynn Rader. After his subsequent arrest, Rader asked the detective, "I need to ask you, Ken, how come you lied to me?" Thank goodness Ken did lie to Rader; otherwise, he'd likely still be living free in his late 70s, having gotten away with some of the worst torture murders ever committed.

The case I'm about to cover bears similarities in the way the criminal acted after committing his depraved acts. He taunted the police and his victims, basking in the fact he'd gotten away with pure evil. But, this time, would the criminal's arrogance be their downfall, or would this be a frustrating case of the killer getting away with it, much like Dennis Rader very nearly did?

To retrace this crime, we have to head back to 1995 in Abbotsford, British Columbia. It was mid-October, and teenagers Misty Cockerill and Tanya Smith were going to a friend's party. While walking to their destination, giddy and excited at the idea of meeting new people and perhaps enjoying some of the free-flowing alcohol, they chattered away loudly. This caught the attention of a man who was already prowling the streets with bad intentions in mind. Terry Driver, a 30-year-old deviant armed with a baseball bat, laid wait in the nearby bushes until he felt it appropriate to jump out on the two 16-year-old girls.

The older, bearded man would already have been a startling sight for the teens, but the aluminum bat he was holding only intensified their panic. Driver asked the girls if they wanted to party. Of course, they did, but certainly not with him. They didn't say this to him, though; they froze with fear, unsure how to deal with this distressing situation. Before they could think of something to say, the man demanded the girls get in the bushes with him.

Their fear forced them to comply. When Driver found a location that suited him, he ordered the terrified teens to remove their clothing. Tanya just wanted to survive this awful night, so she did as the aggressive man demanded. However,

Misty had a different tack; she attempted to fight the man with his bat. She yanked it from him and began raining blows on his back as the attacker prepared to assault Tanya sexually.

Misty had a burning rage in her that allowed her to stand up to the evil before her, but sadly, Driver managed to overpower the girl and take the bat from her. He looked at Misty with wickedness in his eyes before beating her relentlessly with the weapon. As she lay limp on the floor, he hit her again and again. The power that went into these swings saw him beat holes into his victim's head. Once he was done, he dropped the bloodied weapon and resumed his attack on Tanya.

The terrified girl was subjected to an awful sexual assault, followed by the same brutal beating Misty had received. Once Driver was satisfied Tanya was dead, he dragged her lifeless body to the nearby Vedder River and flung her in remorselessly. Unbeknown to Driver, Tanya wasn't dead when he dragged her to the water. She was still breathing, albeit just. She perhaps could have survived the attack, even if the chances were slim. Once he threw her in the river, however, there was no chance for the teenager. She drowned to death to fulfill this foul man's sadistic kicks.

Meanwhile, Misty was lying bleeding out in a parking lot, just regaining consciousness. Driver thought he'd killed her, but she clung onto life, barely. She managed to somehow get her bearings and made her way to the hospital on foot, another miraculous feat. Once there, the medics rushed her in, and the teen could finally breathe a sigh of relief: she was safe. Wounded horrifically but safe.

Her skull was fractured, her finger was bent and broken, as was her arm. Her brain was swelling at a rapid pace - if she'd been left much longer, there would have been no chance of survival. Hospital staff scoured the area to make sure her attacker hadn't followed her there and thankfully found no sign of the baseball bat-wielding man. Misty was immediately treated for her injuries, and a search for Tanya ensued.

It didn't take the police long to find her. It was a sad discovery, though, quickly dashing any hopes of finding Tanya alive. She was face-down in the Vedder, having been unable to muster any strength to remove herself from the water she was thrown into. The hunt was on for a killer.

Fortunately for the police, the culprit wasn't the shy and retiring type. He relished in his crimes and told them as much. He would contact the police and emergency services and admit to being the man they were after. He'd refuse to correctly name himself, but he'd confess to killing Tanya Smith and threaten to kill again. He would crudely detail the vile sexual assault he carried out on Tanya, details only the police, the killer, and Tanya would know: things like the mutilation of one of her breasts. This was never made public knowledge, so there was no doubt in authorities' minds that they were talking to the genuine killer.

They just needed him to slip up in order for them to get any kind of lead. They banked on his ego getting the better of him.

This was proving difficult since the caller was merely using his communication with the police to taunt them that they'd never catch him. He never left any real, tangible new details. He'd also call 911 from a payphone but would flee from the scene before police managed to get there. Likely, he was still around the area when police arrived, watching them hunt for a man they would be unable to recognize. After all, the composite sketch made up of the killer bore no resemblance to Terry Driver. He even gave himself a new moniker - "The Abbotsford Killer." Driver didn't take too much time or any creativity to think of his unique "killer name," it seems.

Driver would continue with his bizarre, deranged behavior as the months went by. He even had the gall to attend Tanya Smith's funeral, reveling in the fact that no one knew *he* was the one who'd ended her life so cruelly and senselessly. He sat through the service undetected, watching her mourning family and friends break down at the unimaginable death of their loved one.

If this act of callousness wasn't enough, Driver took his mockery to new heights when he later stole Tanya's tombstone. He didn't take it as some sort of memento of his crime. He took it to vandalize before leaving on top of a car outside a local radio station. He wanted this abhorrent act to be spoken about over the airwaves; that much was clear.

After this, the calls to the police became more frequent - and more aggressive. He would talk of his new victims, the vulgar things he would do, and the horrific acts he'd already committed.

Ironically, Driver's father was a police officer. This gave Driver an insight into police procedures, something most killers don't often get the inside scoop on. This offered the killer an advantage over law enforcement, allowing him to remain one step ahead of the investigators tailing him. Driver was also an avid listener to the conversations taking place over police scanners and even listened to officers' responses to his taunts of them. There's no doubt the man enjoyed the thrill of mocking the police and his victims, but they hoped his patronizing attitude would eventually catch up with him. To snare the killer, officials released parts of his sneering phone calls to police for the public to listen to, hoping someone would recognize the voice.

It could have been a long shot. The caller may have been using an accent or purposely concealing their true voice. It turns out they weren't: Driver's brother knew it was his sibling as soon as he heard the broadcast. Misty Cockerill also confirmed it was the voice of her attacker, too. Driver's mother also conceded it was her son's voice.

Even more pieces of the puzzle were coming together. Before the phone calls were released, Driver had thrown a wrench through a random person's window. Wrapped around the tool was a note: *from the Abby Killer, call 911*, it read. Of course, the shocked woman whose window it smashed through did call 911. She handed them the wrench that was thrown into her home, which was swiftly sent to forensics. The killer hadn't thought to clean the implement of his fingerprints prior to throwing it, giving the police a nice, unspoiled thumbprint to put in their case file.

The Driver family contacted the police to voice their concern about Terry. He was arrested, and after matching his DNA with the bite mark on Tanya and his fingerprint with the one found on the wrench, he was unveiled as the so-called Abbotsford Killer. However, despite the mountain of evidence against him, including his own family recognizing his voice in the released police calls, Driver denied attacking the teen girls and killing Tanya. He did offer an explanation, though, albeit a see-through one.

According to Driver, he stumbled upon the two unconscious girls while taking a stroll. He then proceeded to sexually assault the immobile Tanya before dragging her limp body to the Vedder and throwing her in. He then explained how he returned to Misty, who was still unconscious, and took her to his car to drive her to the hospital. Despite a hefty case file of evidence to refute this story, law enforcement still had to ask him what made him carry out this barbaric crime instead of helping the seemingly comatose teenagers he stumbled upon. He had Tourette's syndrome, he said, which combined with his OCD and ADD, made him impulsive.

I grew up with a friend whose brother had ADD. It would cause certain issues in his life, although murder and sexual assault were never an issue for him. I also worked in a newsroom with an editorial assistant who was diagnosed with ADD. Again, he never faced the issue of resisting the urge to assault and kill due to his attention deficit symptoms. For me, his counterargument was not only weak, but a slap in the face to people who suffer from Tourettes, OCD, and ADD.

It was an unusual counterargument for a 31-year-old father of two. Before the brutal attack, Terry Driver had flown under the radar as a "normal" individual. The fact his father was once a sergeant in the police also went some way in securing Driver a "squeaky-clean" image.

However, his wife would come forward after his arrest and shatter this illusion. Her husband could be aggressive and ill-tempered, punching holes in the walls if something didn't suit him. In addition to this, her husband often took off for long periods of time chasing crime scenes from conversations he would hear over his police scanner. He would drive to whatever crime interested him the most and observe the police response and crime scene from afar. Sometimes, he'd take his kids on the trip. The image Driver had created of being a kind, decent, family man had crumbled.

Shortly after his arrest for Tanya Smith's murder and Misty Cockerill's attack, Driver admitted to being The Abbotsford Killer. However, at his trial, he reverted to his defense of claiming his ADD caused him to offer a fake confession. His desire for attention, he would say, caused him to make the calls to the police and write fake confession notes signing them off as the killer. The judge swatted away these claims, and in 1997, Driver was handed life in jail for murder and attempted murder.

Tanya's dad, Terry, expressed relief that his daughter's killer and rapist had been jailed for the rest of his natural life but noted it wasn't a joyous occasion: the manner in which his daughter died would haunt him forever. Tanya's mother, Gail Smith, was still too devastated to talk much with reporters waiting outside the court but noted that her daughter was special and loved very much.

Misty's parents also breathed a sigh of relief that their daughter's attacker was never getting out of prison. The fact he'd taunted the teenager by writing "one day, Misty" on Tanya's headstone caused them to fear for their daughter's life.

Surprisingly, Driver's brother, Don, expressed doubt that Terry *was* The Abbotsford Killer. Despite recognizing his voice on the police calls, he didn't believe his sibling was the true killer.

Driver would appeal his sentence, but this was rejected in 2001.

Misty Cockerill has refused to let the horrific day in 1995 define her or her life. She has gone on to obtain a degree in sociology and become an outspoken victims' rights advocate. She recalls the press's attitude to her and Tanya when they reported the crime in the mid-90s. The articles focused on the fact the girls were walking alone heading to a party, not mentioning the fact that the teens had every right to do so without being attacked.

She also recalled how people would comment about what they were wearing that night, not-so-subtly victim-blaming the surviving teen. It was traumatizing at the time, but thankfully, Misty acknowledges that attitudes have changed for the better in recent years. Still, she feels that there is more room for compassion in society, a view I can agree with.

As for Terry Driver, he passed away behind bars in August 2021, aged 56.

A Longing To Kill

All murders are horrific, but there's a distinct emptiness that you're left with after learning about a murder without any real motive. This is one of those cases. The culprit in the case had the world at his feet when he committed two violent murders: a comfortable family life, a financially stable upbringing, and all the freedom an 18-year-old would want.

The more you learn about Steven Pfiel, however, the more you perhaps realize that it's these perceived luxuries that could have been his downfall. When you're spoiled and can have everything you want, going to extremes can sometimes be a way to feel *something*. Sometimes, these extremes are drugs, alcohol, and promiscuity: just pure hedonism. For Steven Pfiel, it was all of these things. Plus, murder and rape.

Born in 1976, little is known about Steven's early childhood. We can but assume it was much like his adolescence, whereby he had rarely been told "no" and materialistic items were freely obtainable. He was, however, known to be a troublemaker with a penchant for violent behavior. At age seven, he'd drop heavy rocks from the overpass onto oncoming vehicles. He was often in schoolyard brawls. He set a motorhome on fire. He was caught chasing another boy with an ax.

As Steven hit his teens, his carefree attitude and recklessness became a concern for his friends. The young man's friends were your typical teens, so it took extreme behavior from Steven to shock them.

One instance occurred when Steven had a party at his parent's home in Palos Park, Illinois. Parties were a regular occurrence at the Pfiel household, and would see parents Roger and Gayle Pfiel retreat to another wing of their house to let the teens enjoy drinking and loud music. On this particular occasion, Steven, after downing beers in the cool nighttime breeze, retreated into the home. He returned only to startle his friends by shooting a shotgun into the sky. While some of the partygoers thought this was a practical joke, some of the teens were unsure if this was Steven unraveling - after all, his behavior wasn't exactly stable at the best of times.

On another occasion, Steven pulled out a hunting knife while hanging out with one of his friends. The friend was understandably shocked at the random weapon being drawn, but what Steven said disturbed them even more: "Wouldn't it be cool to stab someone in the head with this?" This comment was brushed off as another one of Steven's crazy remarks, but in reality, the teen truly was harboring the desire to murder another human being.

There had been signs before this that the teenager was capable of random violence. While listening to music with a friend, he suddenly took a pool cue and began raining blows on the stereo speakers that was blasting out heavy metal until they broke. When Steven was confronted about this after he calmed down, he claimed he had no recollection of the troubling event.

Thrill-seeking was a big part of Steven's life. His friends consisted of what you may call the "stoner" group at school: those who flew under the radar, were unexceptional academically, and used breaks between lessons to sneakily have a quick toke. Steven, however, took this to extremes. He would take acid at the lunch table while his friends laughed at the wild antics that occurred afterward. The gang of Stagg High School students would often skip class, too, preferring to head to the local forest with six packs of beer, some joints, and a stereo.

After an evening binging, one night saw Steven and a pal taking turns driving his car up and down a street at eighty miles per hour while each of them took turns holding onto the car from the outside, seeing how long they could cling on for. Miraculously, no one was hurt.

Steven had been unraveling in front of everyone's eyes for a while, but on July 14, 1993, his sadistic thoughts would come to fruition. There was a midweek party a bunch of people from high school were invited to, and of course, Steven was there. So was 13-year-old Hillary Norskog.

Tiny, unassuming Hillary had just begun looking for independence. The teen had always been attached to her mother's hip, but since she was about to enter high school, she sought to break away from her mom and make friends, attend parties, and stay out late. Her mother, Marsha, knew that the summer of '93 was the one where she had to give her daughter more freedom. She wanted her daughter to grow, to make new friends, and to find her crowd.

Steven and Hillary already knew of one another before bumping into each other at the party. They'd partied together before. On one occasion, Steven was even asked to leave the

Norskog household by Hillary's mother after overstaying his welcome after a gathering there. The pair got on well, with some assuming they were dating. Perhaps that's why, when Steven offered Hillary a lift home that night, she accepted without a second thought. She would never make it home.

He took the girl into the dark of the forest preserve and stabbed Hillary twelve times in a frenzied attack. There was no chance of survival for the petite teen, who would have had time to wonder why her friend was violently stabbing her for no reason. Defensive wounds on her arms and hands proved she tried to defend herself. The majority of wounds were found primarily on Hillary's face and neck areas. Her trachea and voice box had been sliced open. She was unrecognizable by the time Pfeil was done.

This meant upon her discovery a few days later, on July 17, there was no way her mother could accurately identify her - formal identification had to be done via dental records. Still, Marsha knew the mutilated girl was Hillary since she was wearing the exact same dinosaur t-shirt Hillary left the house in on Wednesday night. Perhaps Marsha clung onto a small glimmer of hope that it was just a horrible coincidence and that Hillary was staying with a girlfriend. However, the results came back to confirm that the body was Hillary's, and Marsha's world crumbled around her.

After carrying out the vile murder, Steven simply took himself off home, something Hillary had wanted to do before being lured into the forest. Steven acted normally after carrying out a most abnormal act, and nobody suspected anything - until news of Hillary's body spread through Palos Park like wildfire. As news got back to the Stagg High School students, they all agreed on the same thing: the last person Hillary had been seen with was Steven. This piece of information made its way back to Martha, who immediately called the Pfiel residence to speak to Steven and ask him for more information on what happened to Hillary. Did he leave her in the woods alone? Did she tell him where she was going? Did he have something to do with her death?

But Steven's mother answered the call and refused to put her son on the phone. She told Martha that her boy didn't need the undue stress of speaking with her, accusing the grieving mother of harassing the family. It wasn't just Martha who was looking for answers from Steven; the police were hot on his tail, too. Once the teenager caught wind of this, he headed to the station when officers requested an informal meeting with him. What Steven didn't expect, though, was for authorities to release their specially-trained German Shepherds to search inside his car. These police dogs did their job well, sniffing out a section of blood in the front of the car. It was just a spilled soda, nothing ominous, Steven insisted. However, police dogs aren't trained to look for and alert the police about juice stains, so his story was suspicious at best. A forensic test of the blood speck found confirmed whoever's blood it was matched Hillary's type. The net was closing in.

A search of the Pfeil household ensued, which saw the police find even more incriminating evidence. The clothing he wore on July 14 was all unwashed, piled in his room, and covered in blood. Among his shirt, hat, and even blood-spattered socks was a knife. The teen was cuffed and taken to Cook County Jail. He denied any wrongdoing, but that didn't stop him from staying there for almost half a year until his parents coughed up the $100,000 needed to pay his bail, which was set at a million dollars. Once the ten percent was posted, Steven was free once again. His parents stated they left him in jail for six months for his own protection since locals were baying for blood over the brutal loss of a young member of their community.

The Pfeils made it clear throughout the ordeal that they unequivocally believed their son was innocent and backed him every step of the way. Their insistence that Steven was a victim of a wrongful arrest didn't appease the locals, who knew of all the incriminating evidence against Steven. The hostility from their neighbors caused the Pfeils to pack their bags and move out of town, heading to the village of Crete, Illinois.

Here, Steven had a complete change of lifestyle. No longer did he have a bunch of friends to party with or a school to attend (or bunk off from). He was homeschooled, again for his own safety, according to his parents. The ease of getting drugs had been taken away, albeit unintentionally, and his carefree life was even more boring now. He would still meet with friends when he could, some of whom stood by him and believed him to be innocent. But they were far away now, and it wasn't as easy to attend many parties or gatherings. Still, Steven had his brother, Roger, to help him pass the time.

The pair were close and would often drink together. On March 17, 1995, the pair were left alone in the Crete home, along with their little sister. Roger and Gayle Pfiel had headed out to celebrate St. Paddy's Day in Chicago, so the two brothers raided the booze cupboard and began drinking. Roger didn't have as high a tolerance for alcohol as Steven, so passed out early into the evening. Not ready to end the night, Steven headed to his room to light up a spliff but soon got bored of his own company. He headed back to Roger's room to find him still lying flat out on top of his bed. He stood over his brother as he lay sleeping and made a decision that nobody - even now - can comprehend. He picked up his baseball bat and violently bludgeoned his brother in the head and the rest of his body. Roger awoke mid-attack but was in no shape to defend himself, particularly when the force of Steven's blows was full of murderous intent.

Eventually, Roger lay on his bed, bleeding and convulsing. The attack had stopped. Steven had relented and took off into the kitchen. Perhaps at this point, Roger could have been saved had his attacker called for help. He didn't. Instead, he took a cleaver from the kitchen, headed back to his brother's room, and laid one ferocious chop onto his sibling's neck. Roger bled out. But Steven wasn't done.

He took himself to his sister's room and forced himself upon her. After he raped her, he remained in the home for another few hours after killing his brother and violating his youngest sibling. Little is known about this aspect of Steven's crimes, especially since Steven would clam up about it, but it's speculated that his attack on the girl wasn't short, nor was it just the one occasion that night. Eventually, after hours of perhaps trying to think of a way out of the trouble he was most certainly in, he packed up his father's guns and some camping materials before taking off. It was at this point the sister was able to call the police around 7:00 am the next day.

The police arrived at the Pfeils, but Steven was long gone. However, among the chaos was a handwritten note from the teen. In the note, he confesses to being the perpetrator of two murders. This was the first time he'd acknowledged his role in Hillary's horrific death. His brave sister had to tell the police everything about her ordeal, reliving the painful truth to officers as the hunt began for her wicked brother.

It must have become clear to Steven that there was no way out of this mess. There was a small chance he would have been acquitted of Hillary's murder, but there was zero chance he'd get away with the crimes he committed on March 17. This prompted the teenager to take himself to Michael Einhorn's home, Crete's Mayor. He knocked on the door and confessed he was in trouble. He didn't say what for, but when the police arrived, it quickly became apparent.

Just hours before this, Roger and Gayle had arrived home to find a bunch of police cars and ambulances parked outside their house. I can but assume their first thought could have been that their son had struck again, despite their insistence he was innocent. As they neared their property, which was in disarray on the inside, any speculation they had was confirmed. Not only was one of their children dead, but it was also another one of their children who'd committed the act. Their only girl had been horrifically violated, also by their other child. Their boy, whom they'd just paid a $100,000 bond for, had all but broken apart the entire family. Their boy, who'd just been released on bail for another horrific murder, was responsible for irreparable trauma and heartbreak.

Could this have been prevented?

"Could haves" aren't something I like to dwell on generally, but in cases like this, I feel it's important to look at the facts and see where it went wrong. Based on the facts, you can surmise if you believe Steven's murderous acts could have been stopped.

We know that he was a troublesome child with violent tendencies. His actions were never something he was reprimanded for by his caretakers, something that was still the case when he was initially arrested for Hillary's murder. Even then, he was shielded from facing the consequences of his actions.

Before his arrest, it was clear that Steven was a cruel, unhinged young man. He'd purposefully run over small wildlife when driving, something that his friends didn't scold him for. In fact, some of them encouraged this behavior when riding in the car with him. None of Steven's friendship group saw much wrong with his deviant behavior, even when it came to members of the opposite sex. It was well known that Steven wasn't good at taking no for an answer, which was a rule for him when it came to girls, too. This was shrugged off as typical teen boy behavior by the group.

When Steven became interested in Hitler, he joined a group that idolized him. This was known to his parents.

When Steven was turning 17, he asked for a hunting knife. He was given it for his birthday and used it to kill Hillary Norskog. Steven referred to this weapon as a "toy" to his friends.

It had been reported that Steven had little to no rules from his parents other than to be there when dinner was on the table. Marsha Norskog would go on to file a lawsuit against Roger and Gayle, accusing them of enabling their son's antisocial behavior, ignoring the number of red flags he had shown from being a young boy and gifting him with the deadly weapon used to murder her daughter. The Pfeils rebuked these allegations, insisting they had no reason to be concerned about their son since he had always been a loving boy who had a close bond with his brother Roger. Martha's lawsuit was ultimately dismissed as there is no law against being flawed parents. After the lawsuit, the Pfeils stated that Steven had changed into an antisocial young man because of the circles he ran in. His friends, they say, were the catalyst for him becoming disorderly.

Steven's pre-sentence psychiatric reports are also an interesting read. He had to be evaluated before standing trial to ensure he was fit to do so. His psychiatrist found Steven to be average intelligence-wise, emotionally troubled, showing no signs of mental illness, and calm throughout the interview. However, Steven would become agitated when he was asked about his crimes. Talk of the murders was met with detachment, a distinct remorselessness, and a lack of concern. This mirrored Steven's actions prior to his first arrest. He was fast asleep when the police caught up with him, despite him likely knowing they were hot on his tail. Even when he was bailed out by his parents, his attitude was one of indifference. In fact, he told friends he was sure he was going to sue the newspapers who reported the crime once he was acquitted of Hillary's murder. I can only assume this confidence came from getting what he wanted through most of his life; for Steven, not getting what he wanted just wasn't an option.

After being arrested for his second spate of crimes, it must have dawned on Steven that there was no get-out-of-jail card for him to use this time. The best he could do was avoid the death penalty. In order to do so, he pled guilty to the murders of Hillary and Roger. The assault of his sister charges was dropped at the Pfeil family's request.

The trial began in August 1995. When putting in his guilty plea for the murder of Hillary Norskog, Steven was asked if he wanted to say anything to the court or Hillary's family. Marsha had been expecting an apology for her daughter's murder, although she wasn't expecting it to be said with much genuineness. "No, I do not," was Steven's reply. The lack of remorse was a shock, even to Marsha.

Steven was handed 100 years behind bars for Hillary's violent murder. He remained emotionless when Marsha read out her victim impact statement. She noted how her daughter's murderer had been "coddled" by his parents, even now, as they escorted him to and from court. She glared at Gayle Pfeil as she said this, as Gayle looked to the floor. When Marsha walked back to her seat, she leaned toward Steven's mother and stated, "You knew."

Steven Pfeil got life in jail for the murder of his brother, Roger.

With so much time passing since Steven was sent to prison for the rest of his natural life, we may consider that he's found the guilt and remorse he was lacking as a murderous teenager. He's had a lot of time to ruminate over his actions, and plenty of criminals find repentance while behind bars. While we can't know the answer to this, there is a telling pen-pal request from Steven that may help answer the question. In it, he reaches out to female letter writers, calls himself "lonely and forgotten," and says he's "missed out on so much" while being in jail. According to him, he's been "abandoned by all." No mention of his crime, any remorse he has for it, or his desire to be a better person while living the rest of his life in jail.

The Devil's Daughter

Killer children with an insatiable bloodlust seem to make for good horror movies. It appears evil kids who slay for fun are a popular subgenre of horror, particularly in films made over the last decade or so. These films are often campy and fun to watch. They're typically not scary but instead creepy and eerie. Perhaps they lack the scare factor because we simply can't imagine a child carrying out horrific murders; it seems way too far-fetched for a ten or eleven-year-old to be stalking the streets with murder on their mind. If you think this scenario is improbable, let me introduce you to Britain's youngest female killer. It's not Mary Bell, as many tabloids and books have incorrectly stated as being the U.K's youngest killer, but Sharon Carr, dubbed "The Devil's Daughter" by the British press.

Born in 1981 in Belize, Sharon grew up with three siblings, never meeting her biological dad. The Carr family struggled to make ends meet, but a move to England in 1986 hoped to change the family's dire circumstances. Sadly, there would be more heartache for the Carr's after they settled in Surrey, South East England. Sharon's mother hoped that a move across the pond would alleviate their issues; however, they only intensified. An episode of domestic violence between the parents saw the mother taking a pan of boiling fat and throwing it over her soldier husband. She was arrested for this nasty assault, which saw the end of their tumultuous relationship.

This led to a period of serious instability for Sharon, who was sent to live with a foster family while the dust settled, but she was sent back to her mother within a month. Prior to this upheaval, Sharon had been a pleasant child at school; inquisitive, polite, and helpful. However, teachers soon began to see a shift in the young girl's personality. She became hard to teach, choosing to disrupt the class instead of listening to her teacher. She quickly became the class clown, acting up to make sure all eyes were on her.

Her friends at school were mainly older boys. It appeared that Sharon found it hard to connect with girls, not only her own age but in general. This in itself wasn't a red flag, but her escalating levels of aggression were. It's uncertain what Sharon was angry at. Perhaps she was upset over the fact her mother had found a new partner who already had two young girls of his own. Maybe she was resentful about her stint in foster care. Or, as the facts of this case unfold, it may transpire that the young girl simply harbored an innate lust for murder, one that nobody would be able to stop. Nobody would recognize Sharon's desire to kill. She was disruptive and aggressive, but it seems unthinkable that a pre-teen would be capable of murder, even if they admitted to thinking about it.

In 1992, when Sharon turned twelve, she would carry out a murder that rivals the savagery of most serial killers you can name off the top of your head.

Katie Rackliff was a bright, outgoing, hardworking 18-year-old girl who was working toward her dream career as a hairdresser. She'd just got a job as an apprentice at a local salon. She was earning a little money to fund weekends at the clubs, had a tight-knit group of girlfriends, and was in her first serious relationship. Life felt good for the teen. Until she hit an awfully low period: enduring her first heartbreak. The pain, you might agree if you recall back to your own teenagehood, is undeniably intense. Katie was devastated. She thought she'd met the one, but he broke it off unexpectedly.

To help her deal with the anguish, Katie's friends rallied around and arranged a night out for the young woman, hoping some drinks and dancing would help take her mind off her ex. As luck would have it, Katie's ex was at the same club she went to that night.

The popular spot was called Ragamuffins, and perhaps the bereaved woman was hoping she might bump into her ex-lover while she was there. She took the opportunity to go up to him and see if there was any chance he'd reconsider breaking up with her. He let her down in a harsh way, intended or not: he said he'd moved on, and the girl he was now dating was with him at the club. Katie was overwhelmed with the distress this unexpected news brought her. She felt nauseous, like she'd been hit in the stomach full force. She didn't know what to do or how to act. In a panic, she took off out of the club to gather herself and began walking aimlessly.

Unbeknownst to Katie, evil was lurking nearby in the form of a 12-year-old girl.

Katie Rackliff's body was found the next day. She was laid next to a cemetery, where she'd been dumped by her killer - or killers as police were possibly looking for. Surely, they weren't looking for a prepubescent girl. There would be no way a petite youngster would have the strength to mutilate Katie as she had been. The victim had been stabbed over 30 times; some injuries were inflicted with such force that they went right through her body. The attack was notably sadistic, with a number of the stab wounds being on Katie's genitals. The attacker clearly had a sexual motive, but forensics could see the victim hadn't been raped. She'd been violated, and her sexual organs had been specifically targeted, leading police to believe the killer was an adult man.

The case went cold. Sharon Carr had managed to stay off the police radar due to being the complete opposite of the culprit they were looking for. However, it was only a matter of time before the girl struck again. Or, she may feel the need to brag about her murderous way to friends. Perhaps both of these things would wind up being her downfall.

After the gruesome murder, Sharon went back to school the following week as normal. She was her usual, disruptive self and found herself sent home a number of times for her poor behavior. Still, Sharon's lust for violence persisted, and she was known to hurt animals. As a true crime follower, you'll know this behavior is common in young, would-be killers, and Sharon was no exception. Some of her friends were aware of her twisted acts towards animals, though none ever told her it was beyond disgusting behavior. Perhaps they were too scared, or maybe they knew Sharon would relish being labeled evil. Regardless, the young girl's wickedness was well-known to her peers and the adults around her.

Another girl would soon fall victim to Sharon, two years to the day after she'd killed Katie Rackliff. I can only assume Sharon chose that day because it had macabre meaning to her, not that it was sheer coincidence. On June 7, 1994, the teen was at school in between classes. She spied Ann-Marie Clifford, another pupil, entering the toilet alone. Sharon hurriedly walked behind her, and once she and the innocent girl were alone together, she plunged a knife into her back. Sharon stood and watched as Ann-Marie fell to the floor, her lung punctured by the four-inch blade that had pierced it. Sharon felt pure joy as she saw her victim bleeding, gasping for enough breath to scream as she writhed on the floor. The screams must've alerted some other students as they were walking past the toilet door, and they swiftly entered, seeing Sharon standing over her dying victim.

The five witnesses got Ann-Marie the urgent care she needed. Sharon was simply happy to watch her die. With the critically injured girl on her way to the hospital, Sharon found herself on the way to the police station for questioning.

Bear in mind, at this point, Sharon wasn't a suspect in Katie Rackliffe's murder. In fact, there was no suspicion she'd been involved in any other crime prior to this. Why she attacked Ann-Marie was one of the first questions the police asked Sharon. *She enjoyed it*, she said. *She liked hurting things.*

The officers questioning the teenager were taken aback by how cold she was. She spoke matter-of-factly about the joy hurting her schoolmate gave her. As a result, she was charged with attempted murder. In between being charged and attending her trial, Sharon was sent to an assessment center to ascertain her mental state. As you can imagine, she was found to be mentally unstable, something that was clear to see when she attacked the staff members there.

The trial didn't last long. The evidence was clear cut, and the culprit admitted what she'd done. Sharon Carr was found guilty of actual bodily harm for the assessment center attacks and guilty of the attempted murder of Ann-Marie. She wasn't deemed stable enough to be housed with other criminals in a female prison. Her disdain for other females was clear but was reinforced when she repeatedly attacked the other girls at the psychiatric hospitals where she was detained. Her attacks of sexualized violence toward other girls showed no sign of stopping. While the hospital was trying to understand the motive behind Sharon's brutal attacks, they found nothing they did would stop them. In the end, an unusual decision had to be made: Sharon was sent to live solely with boys at another secure unit. This was the mid-90s, and I don't believe such a move would be made today. However, given Sharon's incessant violence towards only females, the choice to move her here was made to protect the people who had to live alongside her. As expected, the move worked.

After a while, when Sharon entered her mid-teens, she was sent to the notoriously tough Bullwood Hall institution for females. The girls there were uncompromising. The hygiene levels left a lot to be desired. The staff took no abuse. Officials thought Sharon would manage here better. She did. But, unlike other places the teen had been sent to, the staff here were sure to not only keep a watchful eye over the girl but also a watchful ear. Every move she made was looked at with suspicion, although it seems Sharon either didn't know or care about this when she was overheard talking about the murder of Katie Rackliff.

Simply talking about the murder wasn't a crime, but it seemed Sharon knew things about the killing that only the killer would know. Things like what jewelry was taken from the victim. How the victim was stabbed. How full of glee she was that she'd never been caught for the violent murder. Staff at Bullwood informed the police of what they'd heard, and Sharon's room was searched. The police took a few items of interest, one being the teenager's diary. It read like a collection of short horror stories.

The diary had a written admission of guilt from Sharon, noting that she was jealous of Katie Rackliff, and this prompted her to kill her. The journal also exposed the sexual element of the attack, with Sharon admitting she got thrills from stabbing her victim and how she wished she could carry out the murder all over again. "I would make you suffer this time," Sharon scrawled before calling her late victim a "slag." It was clear that the teen hadn't felt one ounce of guilt in the years since the murder. She still felt the same anger and envy towards the girl she'd killed despite already ending her life in a terrible way.

In some entries, she said the devil made her kill. However, she would also refer to herself as the devil. "Killing is my business," she wrote to a friend of hers, "and business is good." In the entry dated June 7, the anniversary of Katie's death, Sharon wrote a sick "tribute": "Respect to Katie Rackliff." The journal was also full of sketches and drawings of murder and violence.

Sharon was confronted with the evidence, notably her own written confession of Katie's murder. She admitted to it without one bit of sorrow. Quite the opposite, in fact; she recounted the killing while laughing. Still, it wasn't straightforward. Sharon would change her story. Then, change it again. In each of her versions of events, the murder of Katie wasn't a question, as Sharon kept this bit consistent: she repeatedly stabbed her until she died.

It's the surrounding events that she kept changing. In one version, she claimed she was with two teen boys the night she killed Katie. Both boys had taken part in sexual activity with the victim before Sharon stabbed her. The killer even offered the two boys' names to the police, but they could take no further action as the teens offered each other an alibi. There was no evidence to corroborate Sharon's story, either. Still, it does beg the question, how did a 12-year-old girl overpower, murder, then drag along the streets an 18-year-old who was bigger than her? The involvement of an accomplice would answer this question, although perhaps we'll never know the true version of events from that night.

The trial began in the spring of 1997. Much like Sharon's earlier trial, deliberations didn't take too long. It was, as before, clear cut. She was convicted of the murder of Katie Rackliff almost five years after the brutal crime took place. She remains Britain's youngest female killer, a title I sincerely hope isn't taken from her in the future. *Isn't Mary Bell Britain's youngest murderer*, you may be wondering. Perhaps technically, that's correct since Mary Bell was 11 when she killed two young boys. Sharon was 12. However, Mary was only ever convicted of manslaughter, not murder.

When sentencing Sharon, the judge remarked how dangerous the teen was, an observation that caused the young woman to crack a smile. Even when her minimum sentence of 14 years was read out, a smile appeared on Sharon's face.

As you can imagine, her penchant for violence and the need to hurt others remained. She was sent to Broadmoor Hospital, a renowned high-security unit that was home to a number of serial killers and violent offenders. Sharon would resume her random attacks on staff here. However, this time, she would also harm herself. She began having thoughts that she was no longer human, that she'd become a lizard. In order to prove herself wrong, she sliced her skin open to see there were no scales underneath. She was indeed human.

Eventually, in 2007, it was ascertained that no medication could help Sharon. They'd tried for well over a decade, but nothing was quelling Sharon's urge to hurt. Still, this didn't stop the woman from applying for her prison status to be downgraded, but this was denied. In her application, Sharon offered no evidence that she posed no risk to others. In fact, her behavior proved the contrary. She was still attacking inmates and staff. She was unable to forge meaningful relationships, and any connections she did make were eruptive, not helped by Sharon's persistent paranoid thoughts.

Sharon's minimum sentence ended years ago, but in all likelihood, she won't be released anytime soon. She shows no repentance, no remorse, no feelings of guilt. Instead, she's expressed the urge to murder again.

This case is an anomaly in the true crime world. Female killers are considered rare. Female killers aged 12 are deemed almost non-existent. Even Mary Bell, who murdered other children at a young age, is now released with a child of her own. The ethics of this being allowed have been debated, but it appears that Mary has managed to develop into a normal adult woman. She certainly has been able to avoid getting in trouble with the law again. For Sharon, the idea that she could do the same gets more and more unlikely as the years pass. She has carried the feelings of anger, jealousy, rage, and violence she felt as a child with her into adulthood, and should she be released in the near future, she would likely take these feelings out on another innocent victim.

A True Horror Script

Murder for money is a recurring motive in true crime cases. Money, it seems, brings out the inner greed in some humans, prompting them to carry out evil acts to get their hands on cash that didn't belong to them in the first place.

Often, it's for a hefty life insurance policy or a rich spouse who gets killed for their big bank account. Sometimes, the criminals in these cases get away with it, living off of their ill-gotten gains. Other times, they manage to squander the money away before eventually getting caught. Sometimes, it's the killer's blabbermouth that gets them captured. In some cases, like the one I'm about to cover, the killer doesn't quite get the bounty they were after. A mere few thousand dollars was all Sarah Stern's life was worth.

In the foggy early hours of a cold December morning in Belmar, New Jersey, an abandoned car was parked on the bridge over the Shark River. The ignition was on, but there was nobody nearby who could be the owner of the vehicle. The long bridge was empty of cars, and no one was walking along it. The taxi driver who happened upon the car felt uneasy enough about his discovery to call the police about the vehicle. It seems the only place the driver could have gone was in the river below, causing certain death, if not on impact, then the freezing temperatures would have certainly killed the individual.

When the police arrived at the scene, they, too, presumed the worst. They traced the car back to Lillian Stern, a 96-year-old woman. Authorities headed to Lillian's, preparing to be met with no answer. If there was an answer, it would perhaps be her husband, and they would have to break the news to the man that his wife was missing, presumed to have jumped into the Shark River.

Once at Lillian's, the woman answered the door, confused as to why officers were there. "Your vehicle is abandoned on the Route 35 bridge," she was informed. Lillian immediately began to panic. She would let her granddaughter use the car from time to time, and 19-year-old Sarah Stern had been using the car for the past few days. She expected her grandchild to be at home fast asleep like she had been.

Sarah was nowhere to be found. An investigation was quickly established, and the police worked to trace the teenager's steps the day prior to her abandoning the car. The Shark River was the first place investigators looked, as it seemed the most likely thing to have happened was Sarah sadly taking her own life. A deeper dive into Sarah's movements the day before the car was found was necessary to discover her frame of mind before she vanished. Police set about figuring out why the young woman felt like the only option she had was to end her life.

Their investigations led them back to Liam McAtasney, Sarah's childhood friend. The police arrived at his home and let them know they were tasked with figuring out Sarah's movements the day before since Liam was the last person to be seen with the missing woman. Liam didn't deny this fact, admitting the pair had spent the day together on December 2. They met up, ate some Mexican food, and hung out for a few hours. "How was Sarah acting, what was her frame of mind like?" an officer asked Liam. The 19-year-old paused and shook his head. "I just know she's been trying to get away," he admitted. This lined up with the police's theory that Sarah had either done something permanent like take her life or made it look like she'd done so in order to run away.

The search of the Shark River was proving fruitless. To some, this was a good sign that Sarah was still alive. To others, there was speculation that she'd have been carried away to the ocean by the time divers got to the scene.

The search then moved back to Liam McAtasney, who'd been friends with Sarah since they met in first grade. Officers caught up with him as he was leaving his house and began probing him some more about Sarah's personality and behavior before she went missing. Liam admitted his friend of over a decade was suicidal and prone to self-destructive acts. Liam said the catalyst for her unhappiness was her father, who would fight with Sarah to the point that it made the teenager want to run away. Sarah's mother had sadly passed away years earlier when Sarah was still a girl, so all she had was her father and grandmother. Canada was Sarah's dream destination, Liam suggested.

Investigators were still at a loss. There was no body to be found, no tangible evidence to lead them to Sarah, and nobody coming forward to say they'd spotted the teen. The case was as cold as the New Jersey winter weather, and it wasn't looking good. The only real lead officers had was Liam, so they brought him in for some more questioning. They pressed for more details but got little more from the teen. All he knew was that she was unhappy before she disappeared. Liam had a question of his own, though: What are the chances if Sarah did jump in the river, that she's floating somewhere in the ocean now?

Police didn't quite have an answer for that but probed the question: did Sarah explicitly say she'd jump in the river? No, Liam said.

They had to let the boy go since he wasn't a suspect and he was offering no new information. A group of volunteers banded together in their hundreds to look for Sarah, scouring the crevices of Belmar and Neptune. Sarah's dad, her school friends, and those who knew her were all present, as was Liam. He brought along his roommate, Preston Taylor. Although they weren't dating when she vanished, Preston had been Sarah's date to the junior prom. Local TV news cameras followed the crowds, speaking to people about their thoughts on the teen's mysterious and possibly criminal disappearance. Sarah's dad told the TV anchor how heartbroken he was. The news crew got Liam on camera, too, his hood over his head and sunglasses covering his face. "Hopefully, we're gonna find something today," he said in a monotone voice.

Despite the large turnout and thorough search, nothing was found.

Nobody knew it, but Sarah's disappearance was a dark plot concocted just a few weeks before her vanishing. Around Thanksgiving 2016, Liam and Preston were hanging out with their mutual friend, Anthony Curry. The trio had been classmates, although Liam and Preston were the closer friends of the group, and Anthony was about to head out of town to work on a horror movie. Gory movies were his passion, as was working in film, so talk of this nature was common among the group.

During this particular hangout, Liam told his buddies that his friend Sarah had found a bunch of money hidden in one of her family's homes. It was old money, possibly forgotten about, and Liam told his friends he planned on killing Sarah and taking the money for himself. *How would he do this*, his friends asked. Liam had already thought about that: He'd offer to help count the loot Sarah had discovered. Then, once at her home, he'd choke the girl out, drive her car to the bridge over the Shark River, toss her over, and leave the car there. It'll look like Sarah ended her life. Talk of how Sarah ought to be killed swirled. A gun or knife would be too messy, leaving too much room for DNA evidence to be left. Choking would be quick and easy, Liam thought.

What about the getaway car? That was Preston's job. He'd use his car to pick Liam up and get the pair away from the crime scene.

Anthony and his friends often spoke about macabre things like this, often in reference to movie scripts he was working on or about horror movies they'd seen. He thought it was another messed up but unserious conversation. It rang no alarm bells for him, and he took off to Brooklyn to resume his career in film.

However, when word got back to him about Sarah's sudden disappearance and the circumstances surrounding it, those alarm bells went off intensely. Everything Liam had suggested - the abandoned car with the ignition left on parked on the Route 35 bridge - had come true. Anthony felt he had no choice but to take this information to the police, which he did, confessing all he knew about the plot Liam had concocted.

Once Liam and Preston had the money from Sarah, they'd split it 70/30, Anthony told them. They'd bury it until the dust settled, but Anthony didn't know how much his friends were set to gain from their crime. By the way Liam was talking, it was hundreds of thousands.

Despite Anthony telling a convincing story, the police needed more solid evidence than this. They enlisted the witnesses' help in trying to snare Liam by getting a confession out of him. Anthony set up a meeting between himself and his friend at the end of January 2017. The meet was just a casual hangout in his car, but unbeknown to Liam, the car had been rigged with cameras and microphones. By this point, Liam had a gut feeling the police were eyeing him up as a prime suspect. He was getting paranoid - and rightly so. When he hopped in Anthony's car, he told him he thought he could be wearing a wire, so he wanted to double-check. Anthony let him feel his torso and pockets for a possible listening device but knew Liam wouldn't find anything - the devices were all planted covertly around the car. The camera was directly on Liam's face.

After checking for the non-existent wire, Liam felt more at ease with his old friend. His guilt spilled out of him at a rate investigators weren't expecting. They didn't expect the coldness at which Liam recounted his crimes, either. But, they had his admission of guilt on camera, a whole 30 minutes worth. "I picked her up and had her dangling off the ground," he told Anthony matter-of-factly. "She just pissed herself," he continued, not acknowledging how this showed how terrified Sarah was.

Still, his attack didn't relent, although killing her took much longer than he anticipated. In fact, he'd timed it on his phone. Just as he grabbed his victim, he activated the timer on his phone. Instead of the three or four minutes Liam had thought, it took half an hour for Sarah to die. When the killer eventually dropped his victim to the floor, Liam said she looked like she was having a seizure. He took a shirt, bundled it up, and coldly shoved it down the dying girl's throat, pressing on her nose to ensure she died.

The hundred thousand dollars Liam had anticipated stealing wasn't even close to the actual figure. The total amount of notes came to just under ten thousand. He was due to give Preston three thousand for being the getaway driver, a duty he carried out. He was disappointed, though Liam still didn't feel too much remorse for ending his friend's life for seven thousand dollars. "What, are you going to live some boring life?" he asked Anthony after confessing he may not even be able to put his ill-gotten gains in the back due to the quality of the notes. "I don't feel any different," he added.

Anthony did a great job of playing it cool throughout, acting as if he was interested in Liam's twisted story, feigning admiration and lack of disgust. All the while, investigators were readying themselves to arrest Liam McAtasney and his friend, Preston Taylor.

Once arrested, Liam refused to talk. It was quite the opposite for Preston; he told the police absolutely everything. How they'd planned the murder, how they'd debated the method of murder, how they'd split the money, how they'd dispose of the body. Preston took police to Sarah Stern's family home to show them how he and Liam moved her lifeless body. Liam took the torso, Preston took her legs, and the pair carried her to her grandma's car before driving her to the Route 35 bridge. Preston even accompanied police to the bridge, explaining how he helped hoist the teenager over the railings before she fell with a loud bang into the river. Preston was subsequently charged with desecration of a body and burglary. As part of a plea bargain, he agreed to testify against Liam, who still wasn't talking.

This testimony and Liam being caught on camera admitting to the murder was damning evidence. Still, Liam denied having any part in Sarah's disappearance.

His defense was that the video was merely an audition tape for one of Anthony's horror movies. It wasn't a genuine admission of guilt, he said. Instead, the teen was using the real-life disappearance of his friend to create a demonstration of his acting abilities, apparently.

Plus, there was no body found. Liam's defense team argued that it was nonsensical to sentence their client for murder when there was no evidence that Sarah was actually dead. Sarah was also known to fight with her father and was desperate to escape. This is the most likely scenario, they argued.

However, Sarah's father took the stand and refuted this suggestion. They were close, and they only had one another. To support his claims, pages of Sarah's social media posts were read out, one of which proclaimed her dad to be the "best dad ever." She posted pictures of his birthday gifts to her, saying how well her father knew her when he gifted her new boots and sweet treats. Apart from Liam's claims of a tense relationship between Sarah and her father, there was nothing else to suggest she disliked him, much less wanted to get away from him.

The jury found Liam guilty of Sarah's murder. He was handed life behind bars without the possibility of parole. Preston Taylor got 18 years for his role in the crime.

What is a life worth? Surely, most of us can't possibly put a monetary value on life. However, some individuals *can* and *have*, and in this case, it was a few measly thousand dollars. You could spend that in a day if you treated yourself to a few luxury items.

If Anthony Curry hadn't spoken up, no doubt Liam and Preston would have spent their dirty money and continued to live a full life despite ending the life of a teenage girl. Sarah was a burgeoning artist, a kind soul, an only child, a chocolate-spread-loving, dog-obsessed, happy-go-lucky girl whose future was filled with promise. For some old, burnt-out bank notes, she was taken from the world in a cruel and terrifying way.

Revenge Gone Too Far

Bullies are a sad but all-too-common aspect of human life. At one point or another, be it during childhood, in the workplace, or woefully at home, we've all encountered a bully. Either we find ourselves in a place where we can remove ourselves from the situation, the offending bully moves on, or ideally, we find the courage to stand up for ourselves. In the case of Bobby Kent, the individuals he bullied all banded together to form a team to exact their revenge on their tormentor. They wouldn't just teach him a lesson - they'd end his life.

Bobby Kent was born in May 1973 to parents Fred and Farah. They set up home in Hollywood, Florida. They were surrounded by sandy beaches, affluence, and year-round warm weather. The family was financially comfortable, with Bobby's father working as a stockbroker. The Kent's made sure their son had the best of everything materialistically, but it wasn't like the boy was spoiled or bratty - to adults, at least. He was a well-spoken, well-mannered little boy who had a way of charming his parents and their friends. However, to his peers, he was the complete opposite. He was demanding, quick-tempered, and frightening if he didn't get what he wanted.

As Bobby entered his teens, his big passion was his vehicle sound system. He spent thousands of dollars making it the best sound system in town and wanted to pursue a career in car stereos. He told his father as much, which pleased Fred Kent immensely. He wanted his son to work for himself, just like he did, and was keen to help his boy achieve his dream. However, Fred saw a few obstacles in Bobby's way that could stop this from happening. Notably, he resented Bobby's close friendship with Marty Puccio, who was Bobby's childhood friend.

Marty had moved from New York to Hollywood, Florida when he was just a boy. The Puccio family moved not far from the Kent's, leading to the two boys meeting in third grade. Frank, however, saw Marty as nothing but a layabout who was going nowhere in life. Not like his boy. Marty's parents also felt the same about the friendship; they were immensely wary of Bobby and felt he took advantage of their son.

As the two youngsters entered their teens, Marty would often return home bloodied and beaten. The Puccios knew that it was Bobby harming their son, but Marty would deny it. Marty's denials, though, couldn't cover up his disdain and resentment toward Bobby, and Martin Sr and Veronica couldn't understand why their son didn't cut his bully from his life.

Marty dropped out of high school, which was another reason the Kents took a dislike to him. They didn't want his apparent idleness to rub off on their entrepreneurial son, and Frank would plead with Bobby to remove Marty from his life. They didn't know that Bobby was using Marty as part of his "entrepreneurial endeavors."

Not only did Bobby abuse Marty physically, he tortured him mentally, too. It was a traumatic bond formed between the pair, something Marty struggled to release himself from. For so long, he'd been Bobby's right-hand man, his punch bag, his gopher. So, when Bobby told Marty they were going to make some money in the adult entertainment industry, he felt he was in no position to decline. Plus, he was a high-school dropout and needed the money. It's not like he could express his uncertainty about the plan. Before, he'd tried distancing himself from Bobby but was threatened with a lead pipe. An incident before this saw Bobby set his dog on Marty, so there was no way out for the young man. At least, that's how Marty felt. So, the pair coaxed a vulnerable Floridian man named Harry Suiter to star in one of their homemade erotic movies.

The plan was for the pair to record Harry naked on camera, dancing, and they'd sell the footage to local adult shops. However, neither Bobby nor Marty were amateur filmmakers - not even close. The footage was grainy, the sound was muffled, and the whole film looked homemade and cheap. Probably because it was. None of the shops around South Florida would purchase the movie, which disappointed Bobby. Still, he wouldn't give up his money-making attempts in the gay market. He would take Marty to the local clubs and allegedly exchange his friend's services for money. There is no suggestion that Marty was a willing participant in this but rather felt coaxed and pressured into doing as Bobby said. Certainly, it's been suggested Bobby made money from the underground sex work culture in Florida, focusing mainly on homosexual men.

As I've mentioned, Marty was scared of Bobby, and his temper was made worse by his avid steroid use. Marty would use steroids, too, but with Bobby already being easy to upset and aggressive, the drug only made him worse. It wasn't only Marty who feared Bobby; just about everybody else in his life outside his family had a reason to be scared of Bobby. His girlfriend was a victim of his nasty temper. She was also a victim of his sadistic sexual side.

Ali Willis would tell her friend, Lisa Connelly, who was Marty Puccio's girlfriend, how Bobby would force her to watch gay adult movies while he violently violated her. While she was initially consenting to this act, Bobby Kent soon took it too far, and when Ali told him to stop, he wouldn't. Ali confided in Lisa about the disturbing things Bobby would do to her, although none of this shocked Lisa. It angered her, of course, but she knew all too well how sadistic Bobby could be. She'd tried plenty of times to get Marty to end the friendship, sick of seeing him with black eyes or a bloodied nose after a beating from Bobby.

To create a divide between Marty and his bully, Lisa was the one to set Bobby and Ali up. She hoped that by doing so, Bobby would have less free time to spend with her boyfriend. As a result, Marty would be free of the beatings and verbal abuse. However, this may have worked marginally, but any aggression and wickedness Bobby wanted to unleash was now aimed toward Ali.

After the incident involving the adult movie, Ali decided to get away from her abuser. She was fearful of him, understandably, so she chose to move back to Palma Bay to live with her parents. Her young baby, whom her parents were taking care of, was there too. Ali was only 18 but had already been married and given birth before she'd managed to exit her teens. When

Bobby learned of Ali's plan to escape, he made it impossible for her to leave. *If she did*, he warned, *he'd smother her baby and then kill her*. Of course, there was no way Ali would risk leaving, especially since she'd experienced firsthand just how violent Bobby was.

Again, she confided in 18-year-old Lisa. The pair were frustrated that this man was hurting everyone around him, and no one was willing to stop him. It has been suggested that Bobby also sexually assaulted Lisa at some point during her relationship with Marty. It's unclear if she told Marty this or if he felt powerless to confront Bobby. Regardless, Lisa felt an inner rage, incensed that her boyfriend's tormentor would be in their lives forever. Just months prior, she'd discovered she was pregnant and wanted to be a proper family with Marty. That would never happen while Bobby was still around. Plus, there was a chance the baby could be Bobby's. If it was, she'd be stuck with him around forever. Marty was the one Lisa wanted, although she found him difficult to attain. He perhaps wasn't as serious about her as she was about him, and Lisa called him her "impossible dream."

Lisa was a shy, self-conscious girl, as are a lot of 18-year-olds. She felt insecure about her weight, something Bobby picked up on. As a result, he would call her a whale to her face, as well as other cruel jibes. Lisa and Ali would sit for hours and talk about the awful things Bobby was getting away with, and the more they did, the more Lisa felt there was only one way out for them. Bobby had to die.

The plan was concocted over a few hours' worth of brainstorming. The pair told Marty of their idea, who was easily convinced it was the right thing to do. After all, he'd been suppressed and abused by Bobby throughout his childhood and all of his adult life. He needed to be free. The trio met up with some more of their friends and told them of their idea to end Bobby Kent's life.

Among the group was 17-year-old Donald Semenec, who had recently begun dating Ali. He was all for ending his girlfriend's rapist's life. Heather Swallers, Ali's good friend, was also invited to listen to the plan. She was all in on getting revenge on her friend's attacker. The 18-year-old had just recently been discharged from rehab, but her desire for drugs hadn't been quelled, which could perhaps explain her complicity in killing Bobby - someone she'd never met.

In the end, they settled with Ali luring Bobby to a desolate area in Broward County under the pretense of having sex with him. Their plan was set for July 13, 1993. When Bobby was distracted with Ali, Lisa was to creep up behind him and shoot the bully dead. Lisa stole her mother's gun to carry out the plot, but upon arriving at the rock pit they agreed to meet at, she backed out of killing him. She'd watched plenty of true crime on TV, so she knew the police could trace the bullet back to her mother. In the end, she decided this tack was too risky. It was back to the drawing board.

The next day, the girls met up to rethink their plans. They enlisted the help of even more people to aid them in ending Bobby Kent's reign of terror over them. Despite not knowing

Bobby, these new individuals to the group were more than game to kill a stranger. By this point, Lisa was desperate for help, so when one of Ali's friends said they knew a hitman, the group was eager to meet him. His name was Derek Kaufman, a 20-year-old with ties to the mafia. The gang met with Derek at his house, hoping he would shoot Bobby for them. However, Derek told them he couldn't acquire a weapon in the time they needed. They wanted Bobby dead the next day. Still, Derek offered his assistance in murdering a stranger. The group agreed and headed back to Lisa's home, where her cousin, also called Derek, was waiting. He, too, joined in on the murderous plot. This made up seven members in total.

The following night, on July 14, as planned, Marty called up Bobby and asked if he wanted to go race cars. Plus, Ali was going to be there, and according to Marty, wanted to sleep with him. Bobby agreed, got ready, and headed out to meet the gang. Meanwhile, the group was getting themselves ready to murder. They'd procured two knives, a bat, and a lead pipe. The macabre plan was simple: they'd meet at the construction site as agreed, where immediately Ali would begin chatting to Bobby. She'd lure him to a private area under the pretense of sleeping with him again. Then, they'd beat Bobby to death.

The plan was going smoothly. Ali had lured the unsuspecting victim to a quiet area next to a marsh. Before anything could happen between the pair, Donald Semenec, Ali's new love interest, ran toward Bobby, whose back was facing him. With a knife in hand, he stabbed Bobby full force in the neck. Stunned, Bobby clutched his bleeding neck and turned to face his attacker. He understood he was at a massive disadvantage.

Still, Bobby knew Marty was around, so he shouted for his friend for help, knowing that Marty wouldn't dare disobey him. Marty did walk out of the shadows toward Bobby, but he didn't offer the help the victim was begging for. Bobby could see Marty had a knife in his hand, too. Out of the shadows, more people stepped forward. The penny dropped for Bobby, who began apologizing to Marty. In response, Marty plunged his knife straight into his tormentor's stomach.

Again, Bobby was pleading, begging Marty for forgiveness. It didn't matter. Marty stabbed again. Bobby turned around and tried to run, blood dripping from his neck and abdomen. The attackers, joined by Derek Kaufman and Lisa's cousin Derek Dzvirko, followed their victim as he tried to escape. Together, using the knives, bat, and lead pipe they'd brought, beat him until he fell to the ground. They incapacitated the man, beating every inch of his body. Still, he wasn't dead, just badly injured. Marty took his knife, lifted Bobby's head from the floor, and slit his throat. For good measure, he thrashed his bully's head on the floor in anger, fracturing a vertebra in Bobby's neck. Kaufman struck the last blow with the bat. They were sure he was dead. It was an intense, violent attack, fuelled by anger, despite half the gang never knowing Bobby to hate him.

The group then carried Bobby Kent towards the marsh and threw his body in. Alligators would feast on him, they thought, before fleeing the scene.

Elation and relief washed over Lisa, Ali, and Marty. Their tormentor was gone for good. Ali could happily move on with Donald. Lisa could have Marty all to herself, and Marty was free to be himself for the first time since he was a young boy. The following day was filled with joy, so much so the killers just couldn't keep what they'd done to themselves. Lisa told her mother what had happened, who then told her sister, who was Derek's mother. The sisters were panicked about what they should do. They didn't want to ruin their children's lives by going to the police, but at the same time, their offspring had orchestrated a brutal murder. Instead of calling 911, they called their brother, who had contacts in the police force. The siblings then got in touch with a detective from the Broward County Sheriff's Office, and the whole twisted tale unfolded.

The first to confess was Derek Dzvirko, Lisa's cousin. He even led detectives to Bobby's beaten body. The rest of the gang were soon arrested and gave conflicting stories. They tried to pass blame and diminish their own, but there was a wealth of evidence against each of them.

Locked up awaiting trial were Marty Puccio, Lisa Connely, Ali Willis, Donald Semenec, Derek Kaufman, Derek Dzvirko, and Heather Swallers.

Heather was handed the most lenient sentence. It was found she ran away when the attack started out of fear and didn't help in the beating of Bobby. Still, she conspired to the murder and was eventually convicted of second-degree murder and conspiracy, landing her seven years behind bars. She was released in 1998.

Derek Dzvirko was found guilty of the same but was given a harsher sentence of 11 years, but only served one year longer than Heather. He was freed in 1999.

Ali Willis was again convicted of second-degree murder and conspiracy, but her jail time was much higher than Heather and Derek's. She was given 40 years for her key role in plotting Bobby's death, although this was lessened to 17 years after she appealed it. She was released in 2001. She's now married with children.

Donald Semenec was also convicted of second-degree murder and conspiracy, but due to his more involved role in Bobby's murder, he got life. He's still behind bars.

Derek Kaufman, the alleged hitman and mafia member, was given 30 years in jail for first-degree murder and conspiracy. It transpired he was neither a hitman nor had an affiliation with the mafia.

Lisa Connelly, after her conviction of second-degree murder and conspiracy, was initially handed life in jail. Like Ali, she appealed her sentence and had it reduced. She was given 22 years and is currently free after her 2001 release. She now has two children and moved away from Florida.

Marty Puccio was convicted of first-degree murder and conspiracy. He remains behind bars and has reportedly found God.

Fred and Farah were happy with the sentences their son's killers got, but Bobby's sister, Laila, voiced her concern when some of her brother's attackers were freed from jail. When the press contacted her, she told them the perpetrators didn't deserve to be alive, let alone free.

The sad aspect of this case is just how little these teens and young individuals cared about human life. They had little to no remorse for ending another life, which was noted at their trials. While it's accepted Bobby was cruel and abusive, murdering him shouldn't have been their first port of call when trying to remove him from their lives. After the messy murder, the gang truly thought their lives were going to be carefree moving forward. There was no gut-wrenching guilt, no sleepless nights, and no terror over the repercussions of murdering a man.

It appears the group, collectively, were incredibly immature, self-centered, and emotionally undeveloped young people. They could not comprehend the irreversibility and callousness of the act they'd planned and committed. Perhaps now they're all older, they've come to realize just how despicable their actions were.

A World Of Cruelty

Foster parents are a much-needed resource in society. With millions of children around the world needing support after their parents pass away or sadly needing safety away from abusive parents, a foster family offers these traumatized children a place of comfort. A foster mother ought to be a figure of safety for such a child. Offering hot food, warm baths, clean clothes, a sympathetic ear, and guidance when needed. Not Eunice Spry - she was the antithesis of a foster parent.

When the 62-year-old woman was accused of abusing, starving, and beating the children she invited into her home over the course of almost 20 years, she denied any wrongdoing. She did admit, however, to the odd "smack on the bottom" of the children entrusted in her care, but nothing more. The evidence against her suggested otherwise.

Spry lived in Gloucestershire, England, where she ran a home for children in need from her house. She had her own biological child, Judith, and an adopted daughter, Charlotte. She opened her home up to youngsters who needed a family, and from 1986, brought in a number of children who were expecting a respite from abuse. Instead, they were entering a whole new world of torment.

The apparent devout Christian took on Victoria, Christopher, and Alloma. In exchange for taking care of the kids, the government would pay Eunice. For her pay, she'd give the children the love, care, and amenities they'd been starved of.

Except, pretty much straight away, Eunice began abusing the toddlers. The horrific treatment only escalated as the kids got older, although it's important to note that Eunice's own children - Judith and Charlotte - were excluded from this poor treatment. On the contrary, they were by all accounts looked after exceptionally well. Sadly, the children who weren't abused were called upon to help abuse their foster siblings, a fact that mirrors the case of Sylvia Likens.

Victoria, Christopher, and Alloma initially went to the local school. Teachers were concerned about the youngsters' persistent bruises and scratches, as well as their nourishment. As per their foster mother's demands, any questioning from teachers about their home life was shut down. *Home life was great*, they'd say, and they were well looked after and happy. In reality, the complete opposite was true.

Eunice was viewed as a pillar of the community. She did a job so very few others could do, she was told by locals, and they admired her for it. To take on others' children, to take care of them like they're her own, and to put aside her own needs and wants was a praiseworthy deed. How different their words would've been if they'd known what was really going on.

Punishment was doled out by beatings. Taking food was considered worthy of having sticks rammed down the children's throats, making it sore for them to cry out in pain much less to eat anything for a while. Plus, if the kids did scream, it was seen as being disrespectful to their mother.

Some bouts of violence were as "punishment" for the children's perceived wrongdoing, but some of the abuse was sporadic and without warning. She'd lash out, encouraging her own children to partake, before locking her foster children in a sparse room together. Often, while locked in the room, they'd go without food and water for days. When Eunice left them for eight days without food, they foraged for rat droppings and ate them. Water was handed to them every couple of days. The children, starving, thirsty, and without clothing, only had one another while confined in the room together, while Eunice and her children enjoyed hearty meals and comfort mere feet away.

A particularly brutal method of abuse the woman liked to carry out was laying the child on the floor, putting her foot on their neck to restrain them, and beating their feet. This would cause the child to struggle to breathe, yet Eunice wouldn't relent in her attack until she was satisfied. Should one of the children say something to upset their "caretaker," she'd squirt washing up liquid in their mouths. By all accounts, saying something to displease Eunice wasn't hard, so having the liquid poured into their mouths was a regular occurrence for the children.

So much so that they began to tell whether they'd had store brand or the expensive stuff squirted in their mouths.

Eventually, Eunice decided to move the family out to the countryside and found an old farmhouse that needed some renovations. She got the property for a steal and was going to use the children to help her fix the place. The kids were surrounded by plenty of lush land, beautiful scenery, wildlife, and a nearby spring. They were also isolated from society. They were taken out of school under the guise they'd be homeschooled. The move to the farm spelled even more abuse for the foster children and separated them even further away from the help they so desperately needed.

The beatings became a daily occurrence. Victoria, Christopher, and Alloma lived in fear of being thrashed with a chair leg, having their legs whipped with bamboo, or burned with a hot poker. The farmhouse was in disarray, with the old building needing much work done to it. Wood, fixings, and metal lay on the floor, ready to be assembled in the decaying house. Eunice, however, used these things as her makeshift weapons. On one occasion, she picked up a random plank of wood from the floor to swing at Christopher, and she hit him across the knees. Perhaps unknown to Eunice, there was a two-inch nail sticking out from the plank, and it had lodged firmly in Christopher's knee.

Despite being paid to take care of the children, there was no running water or electricity at the farmhouse. This caused the children to be dirty and dehydrated, and they had to find imaginative ways to keep themselves warm at night. Of course, the children - or the ones that Eunice didn't favor - were starving. By this point, 10-year-old Christoper felt he had no other choice but to sneak his way into the kitchen to try and get some food for his siblings and himself. As quiet and covert as the young boy was, Eunice stood over him as he rummaged through the cupboards. His punishment took place outside in the nearby field. She tied the screaming boy by his feet and secured the rope to the back of her truck. She got in her vehicle and drove at high speeds around the bumpy grass, dragging the hysterical boy behind her.

Years passed, and life remained the same at the isolated farm. The abuse was a constant, with some particularly nasty attacks from Eunice involving sandpaper to scrub the children's hands and faces raw.

In 2000, Christopher, by now aged 12, was left home with his sibling Alloma, aged 15. Victoria, now 14, was out driving to town with older siblings Judith and Charlotte. In an unfortunate accident, the Spry vehicle collided with a lorry, instantly killing Judith and Charlotte.

Miraculously, Victoria managed to escape the wreckage, although she was placed in intensive care to recover. Eunice had lost the only children she deemed deserving of her kindness. The foster children were the children of the devil, she would tell them and deserve poor treatment. The untimely death of her children saw her acid tongue run rampant toward the foster kids. When she broke the news to Christopher and Alloma, she told them she wished they'd died instead of her girls.

While Victoria was recovering in the hospital and after an invasive surgery to help her walk again, Eunice made sure to blame her for the deaths of her children. *The devil looks after his own*, she told the injured teenager, and that's why Victoria survived. Eunice knew this wasn't true. The man who drove the lorry that collided with Spry's van had been found to be driving recklessly and was jailed for 18 months. Eunice attended his sentencing. Still, she blamed Victoria, whose neck and pelvis had been broken in the collision.

Before she was due to return home after months in the hospital, the doctor told Eunice that Victoria would need some physiotherapy. Otherwise, she'd be wheelchair-bound for months. Eunice wouldn't let the teenager receive the physio, meaning Victoria was forced to be wheelchair-bound, even more at the mercy of her wicked foster mother. Eunice's reason for not allowing physio wasn't just to prolong the girl's agony, but it also meant a hefty payout from the insurance company. The longer Victoria was incapacitated, the more money she'd get. There were also more benefits to be had if she took care of the disabled teen while she was unable to walk.

However, after a few months, Victoria could walk again. But she wasn't allowed out of the chair. Eunice was going to milk this awful situation for as long as she could, and she insisted the girl remain in the chair no matter what. Should Victoria get out of the chair, Eunice would beat her right back into it. This was the case for three whole years, despite the teen - now a young woman - being capable of walking. Eunice stripped three years of liberty from her victim, who had no contacts outside of the home, no way of getting help, and no strength to stand up to her abuser. She lived in fear of her tormentor, and fighting back just wasn't an option. She'd been conditioned to feel as though there was no other option but to endure the hell she was living

Doctors were baffled as to why Victoria wasn't able to walk. She ought to have been out of the wheelchair a few months after returning home. Eunice stopped any doctor who tried to examine the young woman, not allowing them to run tests to figure out why she'd lost the use of her legs entirely. Even dentist appointments were overseen by Eunice, who would never leave her foster children alone with a medical professional. She spoke on their behalf, even as they were heading out of teenagehood.

It would be one of Eunice's fellow Jehovah's Witnesses who finally clicked on to the abuse that was taking place. She visited the Spry home to find wheelchair-bound Victoria covered in red, open wounds on her face. There were too many to count, and the blotches covered her entire face, with some on her neck. The friend took Victoria to one side, who finally broke down and told the truth: the wounds were from sandpaper, and Eunice had held her down and scrubbed her face until she was a bloody mess. That day, she had the courage to stand up out of her wheelchair and go get help for herself and her siblings. Their two decades of torment were almost over.

Eunice, now aged 62, was hauled in for questioning. She denied the accusations, saying she'd never hit the children except for the odd smack on the bottom as a last resort. Investigators noted Eunice was intelligent but cold. Her answers were matter-of-fact, not full of emotion like you'd expect an innocent person to react. Still, she said she loved the children and was a devout Christian who would never carry out such horrific abuse on anyone.

All three of the foster children's stories, as harrowing as they were, corroborated one another.

In the spring of 2007, Eunice was given 14 years behind bars for assault and perverting the course of justice. The judge sentencing her remarked the case was the worst he had come across in his career. The following year, on appeal, this was reduced to 12 years. Eunice was released in June 2014 after serving half her sentence. She's now almost 80 and living free.

Christopher and Alloma, although traumatized and naturally wary of the world, have done their best to carve out healthy, happy lives for themselves. They've spoken of the abuse they suffered, giving the odd interview here and there. Both are well-spoken and have managed to speak about their experiences with great strength. Victoria became a prominent advocate for victims and survivors, working closely with Gloucestershire social services to help them ensure such a terrible case of child cruelty wasn't able to take place again. It seemed as if the three had managed to battle through the trauma and mental scars they were left with at the hands of Eunice. Still, Victoria was said to have been fearful of Eunice's release. She was scared her abuser would come back for her to get revenge.

Tragically, in 2020, aged just 35, Victoria took her own life. Christopher and Alloma blame Eunice for this. Despite Victoria doing so much to help victims of abuse and prevent child abuse, she was struggling with her mental health. In the months leading to her ending her life, she spent some time in a psychiatric hospital. All she'd known from such a young age was anguish and turmoil, and despite her desire to rid herself of this, she succumbed to the years of abuse she suffered by ending her life.

Victoria's siblings and fellow survivors, Christopher and Alloma, don't want her to be remembered for the horrors she endured but rather for the good work she did to stop others from enduring the same.

Injustice

This case could be turned into a gripping court drama - if only it weren't a true tale filled with kidnap, torture, and sexual assault. These terrifying aspects turn it into a real-life horror series. The tale took place in Caracas, the capital of Venezuela, in the spring of 2001. It's undeniably sickening, not only the crime itself but the way the justice system handled it. This case has few details surrounding it, in English especially, so it's a shorter chapter. But it's so unbelievable it has to be covered.

Linda Loaiza was 18 years old, dreaming of becoming a vet and enjoying her youth. There was little for the young woman to worry about apart from your typical teen anxieties. She had a large, loving family and the world at her feet. That world would be turned upside down on March 27, 2001, when she was leaving her home and found herself confronted by a dangerous man: Luis Carrera Almoina.

He threatened to kill her if she didn't comply with his demands. He bundled the terrified teen into her car and took her to a property he owned. As she would later describe it, Linda would experience what it was like to experience death while being alive.

For almost four months, she was subjected to gut-wrenching sexual assaults, frenzied bouts of violence, and unrelenting torture at the hands of her captor. Make no mistake, the prolonged maltreatment of Linda can be likened to that of the

73

Junko Furuta case. The timeline of the abuse she suffered is hazy since Linda lost all sense of time while in captivity. The permanent scars she's left with speak volumes, however.

Luis Carrera Almoina, the son of a politically connected head of a university, caused permanent injuries to his victim. The loss of a nipple. Cigarette burns all over her body. A dislocated jaw. The inability to carry children. A ruptured spleen. He changed the way her face looked forever.

While kept in brute Almoina's property, she was withheld food and water. The assaults she endured occurred multiple times daily. Upon her rescue by the local fire and police departments that summer, malnourished Linda had to undergo a number of invasive surgeries. Not only to restructure her face but to help fix her internal injuries. She spent over a year in hospital recovering from the hell she'd been through. The things she endured are unimaginable, and even if we go to the darkest recesses of our minds, I doubt we could come up with anything as brutal as the four months of torture Linda endured.

What more could happen to this young woman to traumatize her? To be disbelieved and to be refused justice. The beginnings of the injustice and disregard for this case began in the days after Linda was abducted. Her sister reported her missing the day after she was kidnapped but was told there was nothing the police could do since Linda was in a relationship with her abductor. Not only was this untrue, but even if it was, what difference should that make in investigating the accusations?

Linda's sister knew the name and number of her sister's abductor - he was well-known - and handed this information to the police. They called the number, but Almoina told them Linda was his girlfriend. Officers closed the case and refused to investigate further.

After her rescue, Linda sought justice for the horrors she experienced at the hands of Luis Almoina, and even though finances were tight, she began looking for a lawyer who would take on her case. This was a difficult task in itself since the accused's father was a prominent figure in Caracas. The Loaiza family scraped together as much money as they could and eventually found a lawyer who was brave enough to take the case.

The charges against Almoina were rape, kidnapping, torture, and the attempted murder of Linda. *Did Almoina care?* Not one bit. He laughed at the charges brought against him. He was untouchable, he said, because his father knew people. This became apparent when the case against Almoina was postponed nearly 40 times since no judge wanted to participate.

Linda was losing hope. All she wanted was justice and for no woman to suffer at the hands of the monster who disfigured her. The statute of limitations was quickly approaching, and it looked like the judges rejecting this case were hoping it would pass so they could dismiss it.

At a loss as to what to do, Linda went to extreme measures to be heard. She headed to the Supreme Court and stood on their steps, announcing she was on hunger strike until her plight was heard in court. The fact that she'd only recently been discharged from the hospital after a pancreas operation shows just how far Linda was willing to go to get her point across. After years and years of being brushed aside, despite the wealth of evidence she had against her attacker, she'd had enough.

The spectacle caught the press's attention, forcing the court to acknowledge Linda's existence. They finally agreed to give her the trial she'd been asking for. This gave the survivor hope, and for the first time in years, she felt justice could be served. However, when she attended court, she found *she* was the one in the firing line. She was asked accusatory, invasive questions, was victim-blamed, and was held responsible for holding up the trial by being in hospital recovering from her injuries. Essentially, she was re-traumatized by the judicial process. This was compounded by the court making the trial abnormally short.

In cases like this, it would take months to come to a conclusion. After just days, Luis Carrera Almoina was acquitted of all charges brought against him. There truly couldn't have been more conclusive evidence against him, yet nobody was interested in getting justice for the victim. Linda was devastated. Recalling that day, she says it shattered her world. Not only was she up against the man who'd tortured her for months, but she was fighting against a system that was against her. To make matters worse, shortly after the ill-fated trial, Linda was investigated for alleged sex work. Many would have given up at this point. Linda didn't.

She appealed the acquittal. While she waited to see if there could be a retrial, she founded a charity to help support women like her, who'd survived some of the most vile abuse imaginable. Then, a few months later, she got some good news: a retrial had been agreed. She was happy, but she remembered what she was up against before she got too carried away.

It took another half a year, but the second trial took place, and there was a different outcome. Almoina got six years in jail for sexual violence and torture. He was out after a few months. He is still free.

Linda was rightfully outraged. There had been no justice, just the guise of justice taking place.

Linda didn't take this lying down. Plenty would have been so discouraged by this point they'd have to move on. Linda wouldn't and began working on getting a law degree. She graduated in 2011 and now specializes in international human rights law.

Because of this, Linda was able to see the case through to the Inter-American Court of Human Rights, to which they agreed that the State of Venezuela did not comply with ensuring Linda's human rights were met. They advised the State that sexual slavery is a human rights violation and a person - man or woman - has control over their own body.

All of the facts were presented to the court. How Linda had been cuffed the entirety of the time her freedom was taken from her. She was defenseless to stop the constant sexual attacks. The amount of food she had access to was at her captor's discretion. The time she was able to go to the toilet was also chosen by her abuser. The Court eventually found this case to meet the criteria of slavery. A deeper dive into the Venezuelan judicial system showed a distinct lack of training on violence against women at the hands of men. As such, police responses to these complaints were handled inadequately.

Advocates say Venezuela still has a long way to go in regard to creating justice for women. Less than 1% of reported complaints of gender-based violence reach trial.

Linda doesn't dwell on this unfairness despite her attacker not receiving the sentencing she sought out. Instead, she channels her need for justice into other cases of women experiencing violence in Venezuela. She's committed to being a voice for what was, for so long, the voiceless.

The bravery, resilience, and fortitude of Linda is beyond admirable. While she may never get the outcome she wants - and undoubtedly deserves - she's carved a meaningful career making sure she makes a positive difference to the lives of Venezuelan women.

A Thrill Killing

Serial killer fanatics are growing at a rapid pace. There are social media sites, blogs, videos, and groups dedicated to some of the most horrific people to ever commit crimes. This content is made by the adored killers' loyal army of fans. Even serial killers who are no longer alive, like Dahmer and Bundy, have hoards of modern-day "fans." Perhaps these people forget that there were real people who suffered at the hands of these criminals and that their acts caused endless heartache and trauma for the family members left to pick up the pieces.

In some rarer instances, these fanatics are harboring their own murderous desires. That's the case for the disturbing crime I'm about to cover - the violent murders of 87-year-old Oliver Northup and his wife, 76-year-old Claudia Maupin. The culprit in this tragic tale idolized serial killers and made no secret of his desire to become one himself. The killer is a 15-year-old boy, Daniel William Marsh. Don't let his age trick you; he was capable of frightening levels of cruelty.

The story takes place in Davis, California. The city is a popular living location due to its small-town feel, Californian weather, and close proximity to Lake Tahoe and Sacramento. The city feels both huge and tiny; the tree-lined streets give a relaxing suburban feel, and the friendly locals offer warm greetings as you take a stroll through downtown. Crime levels are low, so when Oliver Northup and his wife Claudia were found dead in their home in April 2013, the community couldn't quite believe what they were hearing. Not only was an elderly couple killed, they were murdered in a disturbingly brutal way.

Oliver was a huge part of the Davis community. He was on the school board, was a decorated attorney, and was a member of the Unitarian Universalist Church. Oliver was active in making the city a better place and was still working up until his death. Claudia was also just as keen to make an impact in their local community and was also a member of the Unitarian Universalist Church. The pair had a big, blended family together. Oliver brought six children to their marriage, while Claudia had three children. Oliver also remained responsible for two of his stepchildren from a previous marriage. Over the years, the pair became proud grandparents to 22 grandkids and great-grandkids. Family and community were everything to the couple.

Daniel Marsh would cruelly strip the doting couple away from their family.

Marsh was born in 1997. It feels like I must have made an error when writing the date, but it's certainly correct. Perhaps you can remember 1997 like it was just last year; I know I can, so it feels odd to know that a person born that year went on to become a vicious murderer. It becomes even more surreal when you figure the murders took place in 2013, making Marsh just 15 years old when he took two innocent lives.

As a youngster, Marsh was considered a normal boy until he hit the age of 10. His mother and father's marriage hadn't been stable for some time, but their 2008 divorce really affected Marsh. His mother had left his dad for another woman, something the child found hard to deal with. His mother, Sheri, would say her son's resentment and anger could have presented itself, in part, due to him witnessing his father's short fuse and verbal abuse.

Sheri says she left the marriage due to her husband's refusal to change and the fact her children were clearly quiet and tense around their father. To offer them some stability, she moved out and moved on, but her son would outright refuse to acknowledge his mother's new partner. Marsh's sister was the opposite. While Sarah elected to live with her mother full-time, Daniel would split his time between homes. It was also around this time he began thinking dark thoughts: fantasies of torture and hurting people.

The shift in Marsh's personality didn't go unnoticed, so he was sent to a therapist. In these sessions, he confided that he wanted to kill people and that these weren't just fleeting thoughts; he truly wanted to act them out. As a result, the boy was diagnosed as being depressed. In 2010, aged 12, he was placed on strong antidepressants, taken twice a day.

As you may expect, Marsh's instability and dark thoughts weren't quashed by the antidepressants. Like many children who suffer from mental struggles, he sought out alcohol and drugs from a young age. The only difference, from what I can tell, is that most children who have dark thoughts don't want them. They seek out these things to distract them from their struggles. Daniel Marsh seemed to enjoy his violent thoughts and made no secret about the fact he would like to be a serial killer.

Marsh's dad got sick of his son's drug and drink usage and threw him out. The now-14-year-old had no choice but to retreat to his mother's home, although Sheri couldn't tell that her son was abusing substances. Perhaps, in part, this was due to him distancing himself from her in the years prior, so she would have no solid idea what her son was like anymore. Regardless, his behavior was spiraling, and his violent desires became even stronger.

At one point, the teen admitted some of his thoughts to the school counselor. He told of his urge to kill, which saw the police come to the school and detain the boy, who was then placed in a psychiatric hospital. Upon his eventual release and a change in medication, Marsh went back to school and repeated his desires to the counselor. This time, his fantasy had become more graphic: he wanted to torture his schoolmates. When asked how he would carry this out, Marsh went into gory detail. First, he'd peel their skin off. Then, he'd slice off their eyelids.

This time, though, the police weren't alerted. For some reason despite Marsh admitting he wanted to carry this violent act out, the counselor felt the boy didn't have any real intent on killing anybody. As we now know, that was wildly incorrect.

Daniel Marsh was free to walk the school corridors, eyeing up his peers, wondering what it would feel like to pull their flesh from them. In class, he'd daydream about bringing a firearm into his school and blindly eliminate anyone in his path. A massacre was something he thought about a lot, and he even opened up to friends about it. Of course, other 14-year-olds will have thought their friend had just watched too many horror movies or that he was making a dark joke about disliking his classmates. But Marsh wasn't kidding.

As the school term went by, his talk of murder escalated and became more frequent. He'd draw gruesome sketches of murder and share them with his friends. "If I got caught for murder, I'd just plead insanity," Marsh would say, much to his friends' amusement. However, what they thought was a joke was very much a genuine thought for their wayward friend. Perhaps this became more apparent when Marsh showed off his murder plan for his girlfriend's ex. He noted how he was going to kill him, being meticulous in his descriptions.

As most killers do, Marsh engaged in acts of animal cruelty. At one point, the brazen boy asked one of his friends if he could kill his dog. Again, I can but assume his friends thought he was joking. If not, this case has as many red flags as the Steven Pfiel case I covered earlier. This tale, just like the Pfiel one, could have possibly been prevented if the bright red flags had been spotted as they continuously appeared, one after the other. It was also known that Marsh liked to frequent a website dedicated to real-life gore. I won't name the site, but it depicts horrific true photos and videos of horrible things happening to people. For Daniel Marsh, this was his favorite form of entertainment.

When Marsh was 15, in 2013, he would eventually act out the fantasies he'd been telling people about all these years. He no longer just wanted to consume gore - he wanted to be the one carrying out the attack. On April 14, that's exactly what he'd do.

The boy waited until the early hours and took himself off through the darkened residential area of Davis. He'd planned his attack carefully. He slid a hunting knife into his belt. He made sure his outfit was only black. He wore a balaclava. He slipped on gloves to prevent any fingerprints from being left. The only thing he hadn't planned was who the victim - or victims - would be. That conundrum was soon solved when he arrived at Oliver and Claudia's home and used his knife to break their window screen. Marsh didn't know who was inside but that didn't matter - he knew he was going to kill them.

He jumped through the window and found himself in the home's living area. Unfamiliar with the layout of the home, he stayed put until he heard a rumbling sound coming from the stairs. It was snoring. Marsh followed the noise, and it led him to the elderly couple lying next to each other in bed, sound asleep. The pair had no idea that a murderous 15-year-old boy was standing above them, contemplating the best way to end their lives. Marsh would later describe this experience - the voyeuristic thrill of watching his prey before lunging - a "exhilarating."

If you're anything like me, when someone enters the room or stands above you while you sleep, some kind of sense alerts you to their presence and wakes you up, often with a jolt. This was the case for Claudia, who awoke to Marsh staring at her, knife in hand. She barely had time to scream before he pounced on her and stabbed her time and time again in her abdomen.

There was no hesitation on the boy's part, repeatedly striking the woman and piercing her with the knife. The more she cried, the more frenzied his attack became. She was resilient, however, something Marsh didn't expect. He had to stab her more than he assumed, possibly believing her to be frail due to her age. When Oliver awoke due to the screams of his wife, he too was subjected to multiple stab wounds - over sixty.

Marsh wasn't done yet. His victims were dead; there was no way they'd ever have survived the prolonged and excessive number of wounds they suffered. Still, he was intrigued by what he'd just done and desired to mutilate his victims. He took the knife he'd just used to violently end their lives and cut Oliver and Claudia open. He removed their organs, disemboweling them in the process. Macabrely, he made a botched attempt to remove Claudia's eyes, something he was unable to do. The boy then decided to place random items inside the couple's bodies. He also mutilated Claudia's leg.

When he was done, Marsh cleaned up to make sure he left no trace of himself at the crime scene before taking off.

The twisted teen returned home and lived life normally. In fact, he was happier than before, with his somber mood seemingly lifted. Nobody but Marsh knew why. His grades at school even began improving. However, the month after the murders, Marsh was sent home from school upon being found with a hunting knife.

Meanwhile, the city of Davis was rocked by the disturbing killing. The couple's sickening murder was discovered after Claudia's daughter became concerned about the lack of contact with her mother. She called the police, who accompanied the worried woman to her parent's home. She peeked through the window that had been sliced open and noticed specks of blood. The police took charge to inspect further, making the horrific discovery.

Forensics attended the scene swiftly, but frustratingly for everyone, the killer or killers left no DNA or any tangible evidence whatsoever. In fact, if it weren't for the killer's arrogant need to brag about his crime, it's likely he'd not have been caught at all.

The day after the murder, Daniel Marsh gloated to a friend about carrying out the barbaric killing. He tried to impress his girlfriend by asking if she'd heard of the murder; when she said she hadn't, he told her in great detail how he killed the couple. It wasn't just matter-of-factly, either: Marsh relished his recollection of the event, describing it animatedly with a smile on his face. His girlfriend knew Marsh was prone to tall tales and exaggerations. Plus, he liked gore, so a twisted murder in their town was bound to pique his interest. Thus, none of his confessions were taken seriously.

However, Marsh's need to brag about the murders took over, and any opportunity to recount his evil deeds to friends was taken. Eventually, to prove he was telling the truth, he showed a friend the outfit he wore the morning of the murders, as well as the murder weapon. As he showed off the evidence, Marsh chillingly explained how it was "the best feeling of his life" killing the elderly couple.

You would be forgiven for thinking Marsh's friend headed straight to the police with this information. He did not. Neither did his girlfriend, who also now knew her boyfriend had been telling the truth when admitting to the killings. However, the teenage girl now felt uneasy around her boyfriend, and who could blame her? By the beginning of June, around six weeks after the murders, she mustered up the courage to end the relationship.

Of course, Marsh didn't take this well and stewed in his anger for a few weeks before breaking into her home one night, just like he did the morning of April 14 when invaded Oliver and Claudia's home. As you can imagine, this was a nightmare scenario for the young girl. No doubt she thought she was going to be victim number three, but thankfully, she managed to defuse the situation and got her ex-boyfriend to leave.

The teen girl was shaken by the incident. She truly felt she was in danger, and she wasn't wrong. She opened up to a friend about the break-in and even admitted that Marsh was responsible for the murders that happened in April. This caused more people in their friendship group to learn of Marsh's involvement in the crime, news that got back to Marsh's friendship group.

While most of his friends were fearful of him, hence the reason they hadn't been to the police about his admission of being the murderer, one of his friends took the troubling information to Daniel Marsh's dad, who did nothing with this knowledge. He said he didn't believe the teenager. Although disheartened by the lack of support, this didn't stop the youngster from taking his story to the police. After a grueling interview with officers on June 16, 2013, the boy offered them all the info he had about Marsh and the horrific murders months prior. Marsh was arrested the next day.

While he was full of bravado and glee during the aftermath of the murders when he was in the interview room, he cried and wept his way through the interrogation, denying any involvement with the violent crime he was accused of. Marsh begged the officers questioning him to believe his story, but when it became apparent they did not, he changed tack. Almost four hours into the interview, 15-year-old Daniel Marsh admitted to the murders of Oliver Northup and Claudia Maupin. When asked why, he said he lost control that day and felt he had to carry out a murder - it didn't matter who the victim would be.

As the police talked more with the teenager, the boy admitted he enjoyed the killing. Not that there was belief Marsh was lying, but if there was, it was soon eradicated when he recounted with no remorse the terrible things he did to the couple after killing them. It gave him a feeling of pure happiness, he said. The best joy of all, Marsh said, was when his elderly victims were conscious, and the attack was taking place. He liked that they knew what was happening, their futile resistance, and the feeling of power.

During the lengthy interview, Marsh told one of the officers how he would kill him, should such an opportunity arise: perhaps he'd smash his face into a mirror and then cut his throat with the broken glass. Maybe he'd gouge his eyes out. Although Marsh reminded him, it wasn't anything personal - he felt zero empathy for other humans, and his desire to kill consumed his thoughts.

With the confession in the bag, Daniel Marsh was charged with two counts of murder. Despite his admission of guilt, he decided to plead not guilty due to insanity. His plea was rebuffed when he was assessed by a psychiatrist who deemed him sane, although he did acknowledge the teen had mental health problems.

The trial began in September 2014, almost a year and a half after the murders. Marsh's defense hinged largely on the fact he was on antidepressants, which had nasty side effects. The pills he was on and the dosage caused the teen to fly into fits of rage, as he did when he took off in the early hours of April 13, 2013, in search of someone to kill. It was his medication, the defense team argued, that resulted in Marsh becoming temporarily insane, resulting in the murders. This could have been an argument that held weight if it wasn't for the mountain of evidence against the now-17-year-old.

Not only were there a slew of witnesses to give Marsh character references, including his ex-girlfriend but there were also testimonies from the therapists who'd been working with him since his arrest. He'd even threatened to kill one of his psychiatrists. Factor in how premeditated the murder was - Marsh had everything in place, bought the tools he intended to use to murder someone, and had a plan to ensure he left no DNA at the crime scene - then it's hard to swallow the idea he was temporarily insane.

It was of little surprise that Daniel William Marsh was found guilty of two murders in the first degree. Due to his age, the death penalty was never an option. He was sentenced to 52 years in jail before he could apply for parole. However, this sentence is overruled by a law in California that states juveniles serving life ought to be eligible for parole after serving 25 years of their sentence. This would mean Marsh could be in his early 40s when he's released. As you can imagine, this caused the families of the victims - who are also victims of this crime - to face another wave of upset and heartache.

In the years after Oliver and Claudia's murders, the family did their best to deal with the trauma of the aftermath. However the bereaved children and grandchildren suffered bouts of depression and anxiety, particularly Oliver's son, whose Lou Gehrig's disease flared up badly after learning about his father' brutal death. In 2018, they were shocked to discover Marsh had given a talk and uploaded to a video-sharing website, where he gave a motivational speech. In this talk, he described himself as "damaged" but insisted he was reformed and deserving of another chance. The video lasted no more than 48 hours online before Oliver's and Claudia's families collectively banded together to get it removed. You can no longer find it online.

Daniel Marsh remains behind bars in San Diego.

Evil Infatuation

On January 10, 2019, Jeanne Nutter was out walking her Labrador in the woodland near her home in Gordon, Wisconsin. It was freezing out, so Jeanne had a big coat and some warm boots on for the routine walk. It was a shock for her, then, to stumble upon a girl wearing just a light sweater and leggings, trying to run in shoes clearly far too big for her small feet. She must have left the house in a hurry, she thought.

"You've got to help me," the distressed girl cried out several times. Stunned, Jeanne made her way to the girl, and as she got closer, it hit her like a brick: *she knew who exactly this girl was*. She'd been all over the news for months, almost three, in fact. She'd been taken from her home in the early hours by an unknown captor. She was 13 years old, and her name was Jayme Closs.

Three months earlier, on October 15, 2018, James and Denise Closs were fast asleep, as was their only child, Jayme. They had no idea of the evil that awaited them outside their house. A 21-year-old man had become obsessed with Jayme, a quiet and shy child he'd spotted getting on the school bus. It was at that moment he became infatuated with the child and decided he was going to kidnap her. He found out where she lived, figured out her mother and father's routine, and gathered Jayme was an only child. He would drive his car to the property at night and wait outside. His name was Jake Patterson, a loner and former marine. He was viewed as shy and quiet, but nobody could ever presume the depths of depravity the young man would end up going to.

On October 5, 2018, Patterson decided it was time to take his young victim. I don't believe Patterson thought of Jayme as his victim, however; I think he was delusional and believed he could take her and make her fall for him. Still, he wasn't mentally ill and knew what he was doing was wrong. He suppressed the knowledge that it was twisted and wrong. He drove to the Closs family home but could see some movement inside. This spooked him from entering the property as he'd planned. Still, he came back a few days later, hoping to sneak in, capture the girl, tie her up in the trunk of the car, and drive off with her. Again, he saw Jayme's father was awake and took off. Patterson was afraid that if someone saw him, he'd be identified.

Witnesses were proving to be a problem for the soon-to-be kidnapper. So, to remedy that issue, on October 15, he returned to the Closs's with a shotgun. Just before 1 am, Patterson rolled up to the family's driveway. This wasn't an off-the-cuff decision. The man had bought himself a ski mask and donned a black outfit to disguise himself, as well as the firearm. He had ample time to stop what he was doing and seek help for his obsession with a young girl, to prevent himself from carrying out his urge to kidnap the youngster who'd never even spoken to him. Patterson was, however, intent on carrying out the abduction of Jayme Closs.

Jayme noticed a strange figure lurking outside and headed in the pitch black to her parent's room. "There's somebody outside," she whispered to her father. James Closs got out of bed and headed to the front door to see who was hovering around their home in the early hours. As James approached his front door, he shone his torch to get a better look at the man. Patterson demanded James open the door, which, of course, the father of one declined to do. Patterson shot James through the door, shattering glass and shooting the man straight in the face. The shot was fatal. Patterson's plan was working perfectly; he'd just gotten rid of his biggest and toughest obstacle, the father.

The killer scoured the home, searching for his victim.

While he did, Denise Closs had managed to make a phone call to 911. The call was barely audible, and the handler was unable to make out much of what Denise was saying. The chilling call was mostly screams and sobs, resulting in a police car being dispatched to the Closs house. The call was made while Denise and Jayme were huddled in the bathtub together, hoping to hide from the intruder until he left with whatever he wanted. They didn't know that what he wanted was Jayme.

Patterson eventually made his way to the bathroom. It was locked, but it was no match for his shotgun.

He blew the door open and saw Denise with a protective arm over Jayme, screaming at the intruder to leave them alone. Jayme was terrified and was crying loudly. Patterson made Denise tape her daughter's mouth shut.

Patterson overpowered both mother and daughter and used duct tape to restrain Jayme while he shot her mother to death. Bound at the hands and feet, Jayme was unable to move. Patterson didn't carry his victim to his car but instead dragged her through the house, past her badly disfigured father, through the shards of broken glass - almost slipping on James Closs's pool of blood - and flung Jayme into his trunk. He sped off into the night as the police were almost at the Closs residence.

In fact, on the drive to Gordon from Barron, which is about 66 miles, Patterson passed the police car that was making its way to the Closs's. He pulled over to let it pass, then resumed his journey to his cabin. Once they arrived, the kidnapper marched the teen girl inside, forced her to change into a pair of pajamas he'd taken from his sister, and warned her he'd hurt her if she tried to flee.

Meanwhile, the police were greeted with the horrific double murder scene. They found James Closs, his face taken off from the shotgun. They searched the property, finding another disturbing sight in the bathroom. Denise was laid in the bathtub, bathing in her blood. She was dead. Immediately, the police knew they were missing a person.

Jayme was forced to lie down under Patterson's mattress and go to sleep. The girl, of course, didn't sleep but kept as quiet as she could so she didn't upset her captor. Patterson set about burning Jayme's clothes to get rid of any evidence. He made sure there was no way of getting caught. Even though Patterson only took four minutes from entering the Closs house to kill the parents and take Jayme, he still managed to retrieve the spent shotgun shells he used in the murders. He'd also shaved his head in preparation for the day of the abduction, fearful of leaving any stray hairs at the crime scene. This is a perfect example of a crime that was *not* carried out on impulse.

The search was on for Jayme. The story of her parents' horrific deaths was on the local news frequently, as were updates - or lack of them - about her disappearance. Her picture had been etched in the minds of the residents of Barron, her image on the front page of the papers along with her parents. The community was shocked at the brutality of the crime and was desperate for the young girl to be found alive. The killer had been clever, though, and there were no leads, no witnesses, nothing at all for police to cling onto and investigate. As the days passed, statistically, it was looking less and less likely - getting close to a zero chance - that Jayme was going to be found alive.

A week after the murders and abduction, the police were alerted to a break-in at the Closs house. You may already know that some criminals like to return to the scene of their crime, either to bask in the horrific things they've done or to collect a twisted memento. It was the day of James and Denise's funeral, so the killer perhaps felt it a fitting day to return to the place where he slaughtered two innocent people. Authorities expected this to be the case and quickly made their way to the home. Inside, they found 32-year-old Kyle Jaenke-Annis taking some of Jayme's clothing, including her underwear and dresses.

He was cuffed and brought to the Barron County Sheriff's Department. They believed they'd caught the killer and were one step closer to finding Jayme.

After questioning the criminal, it became clear he wasn't anything to do with the murders and abduction. He was a small-time, albeit strange, crook who was looting the scene of a gruesome crime. The police, who felt they were about to crack the case, found themselves without any clues yet again.

Jayme was still at Patterson's cabin in Gordon. He would occasionally let her out to stretch her legs, but only after he'd scoped the area to make sure no one was around. His rule over Jayme was by fear, so much so he didn't make much of an effort to keep her from escaping. If he had to go out, he'd force the girl under his bed and enclose her there using items of furniture. Not exactly escape-proof, but Jayme heeded Patterson when he told her he'd hurt her if she tried to flee. Not that this stopped her from thinking about escape; she was just waiting for the right time. She'd been evaluating his routine, getting to know him, understanding the brute who was forcing her to share his bed at night.

Little has been revealed about what truly went on inside the cabin. There have been no charges of sexual abuse brought toward Patterson, and from the brief descriptions of life inside the cabin, it seems like Patterson was keeping his obsession as a companion. He'd have Jayme sit next to him as they watched TV, bring them board games to play, cook food, and he'd speak to his captive like she was his friend.

An agonizing 88 days passed, and the news stories of Jayme were trailing off. It was presumed, sadly, that the worst-case scenario had come true, and the teenager had met the same fate as her parents. Until the police received a panicked 911 call from dog walker Jeanne Nutter, explaining she'd found Jayme. You can imagine the call handler wasn't exactly convinced at first. "Have you seen Jayme's picture," she asked Jeanne, who said yes, she'd seen it all over the news - it was Jayme, and the girl herself said so. In fact, she also had the name of the man who'd murdered her parents and had been keeping her hostage for three months: Jake Patterson.

Jayme had waited until her captor said he was going out. She knew he'd be gone a while, so she decided she was going to take her chances that day and make a run for it. He thought he'd made the girl so fearful of escape that she wouldn't bother trying, so he neglected to lock her in. Seizing the opportunity for freedom, Jayme pulled on a pair of Patterson's sneakers and raced out of the door. It wasn't long before she spotted Jeanne and flagged her down, desperate for help.

It didn't take long for the police to find Patterson driving his car. They pulled the 21-year-old over and got him in the back of the patrol car. By this point, officers had picked Jayme up from Jeanne's and drove her out of the Gordon area to ensure her safety. After all, the cabin she'd been kept in was a mere few houses away, and the man who did this was clearly unhinged. There was no telling what he'd do. It came as a surprise to police, then, when they had Patterson in the back of the car and found him to be calm and cooperative. Still, the man was responding oddly to being arrested. He was more concerned about who would turn his car engine off and take care of his vehicle. He also complained about discomfort in the back of the police car ahead of the long drive to the station.

Despite his blasé attitude, he must have known the net had well and truly closed in; there was no getting out of the trouble he was in. A full confession spilled out of Patterson. The murders, the kidnapping, even telling police they drove past him as he sped away with Jayme in the trunk the morning of the crimes. He stressed, though, that he never touched her sexually. He said it was about companionship, and that was it.

The prosecution didn't want to force Jayme to endure a trial, so no sexual assault charges were ever filed against Patterson. We'll never truly know what went on in the cabin without making Jayme relive it in front of the court, something she never wanted to do. Understandably, she just wanted to get on with her life. The first thing she said after her escape was that she wanted to go home. Her home, tragically, would no longer be with her mother and father. She went to live with and remains with her Aunt Jennifer.

The store where Jayme's parents worked had put up a $25,000 reward for anyone who could lead them to the girl. Since she'd rescued herself, they gave Jayme the money.

In the spring of 2019, Patterson's trial began. To avoid hauling his victim through a traumatic trial, he said, he pleaded guilty to two counts of first-degree homicide and one of kidnapping. Initially, armed burglary was on his rap sheet, but this was later dismissed.

While in jail awaiting sentencing, Patterson wrote a letter to a local reporter. He said he committed the crimes on impulse and was sorry for them. It's hard to believe that he acted impulsively since he'd clearly planned the kidnapping some months before carrying it out. The fact he sought out a shotgun and brought it with him on his third kidnapping attempt is also suggestive that he fully intended to kill the Closs parents. He'd also stolen his sister's pajamas for Jayme to wear prior to abducting her.

In May of that year, Patterson was sentenced to two life sentences in prison for the murders plus 40 years for the kidnapping of Jayme. He will never be eligible for parole. The judge sentencing him said he didn't know how Patterson could be rehabilitated from his twisted thoughts and ideologies.

Jayme wrote a victim impact statement, which was read out in court. In her letter, Jayme explained how the most important things in her life were her parents and her home. For his own sick desires, Patterson had evilly stripped this away from her. Jayme's aunt spoke on her niece's behalf, stating that the teen was focusing on getting on with her life day by day, and would very likely have more to say on the tragic events as she gets older.

In June 2019, Patterson registered as a sex offender despite never being charged with any sex offenses against Jayme. Again, little was mentioned about this aspect of the sick crimes to spare Jayme the re-traumatization of a trial. His addition to the offender's register is telling, though. Since he'll never be released, the prosecution didn't push for this aspect of the abduction to be on his rap sheet.

Jayme's strength, mental toughness, and determination to live are beyond admirable, and I pray those attributes remain with her as she reaches adulthood.

Murder For Motherhood

There's an extremely rare category of crime called "fetal abduction." You may not have heard of it before, but you can likely guess what it entails from the name. Essentially, it is the criminal act of a person - in most cases, a woman - kidnapping or attacking a pregnant woman with the intent of removing their baby via improvised cesarean section.

Bear in mind that the perpetrators of these crimes aren't surgeons; they don't use sedation or pain relief, so removing the child (should the mother be awake during this) would be horrific. *Why would anyone do such a thing*, you might wonder.

Often, the perpetrator is unable to get pregnant and fake their pregnancy in the months leading up to the fetal abduction. They either gain weight or use a fake pregnancy bump to fool friends and family into believing their lie. This aspect I can sympathize with; to be unable to become pregnant despite it being your greatest wish in the world is beyond soul-crushing. The wicked aspect of this crime comes when the perpetrator actively seeks out a pregnant victim to murder for her baby. That is an unfathomable act.

But it happens, and one such case was the murder of Reagan Michelle Simmons-Hancock, a 21-year-old from Bowie County, Texas, in 2020.

Reagan was already a mother of one but had recently fallen pregnant with her second child, who was to be named Braxlynn Sage. The little girl was already so loved before she entered the world, and Reagan was looking forward to caring for another baby.

Her other daughter had turned three and was quickly getting older, already having back-and-forth conversations with her mother and showing curiosity for everything around her. The young mother had a sturdy support system, with her sister and mother ready to lend a hand with the youngsters. She also had a few close friends, one of whom she'd just recently met, fellow mother-to-be, 29-year-old Taylor Rene Parker.

What Reagan couldn't know was that Taylor wasn't pregnant at all. Her new friend wasn't able to carry a child since she'd had a hysterectomy. Taylor already had two children of her own but wanted another with her boyfriend, who she was afraid would leave her if she couldn't give him a baby. She felt unable to tell him about her hysterectomy, instead withholding this information and lying about her ability to conceive.

In the months leading up to the gruesome murder of Reagan, Taylor had been looking into how she could make it seem as if she was pregnant. She looked into how to deliver babies at home, searching the internet to find videos on home births. She wanted to know exactly how to do it since she was planning on finding a pregnant woman and forcing them to hand over their baby. She just needed to find someone who fit the bill, and after telling her boyfriend they were expecting, she had to find a victim quickly.

How Reagan and Taylor met is unclear, but we know it wasn't by chance. Reagan was exactly what the woman had been looking for, and she quickly chose her to be the victim whom she'd rip the baby from when the time was right.

In the meantime, Taylor was gleefully telling those around her she'd fallen pregnant. Her family was elated, as was her boyfriend of 10 months. She'd hand out ultrasound pictures, pointing out what features the baby shared with the father. Of course, this was just another way for Taylor to keep up the wicked ruse. A part of me feels sorry for the woman not being in her right mind with the frustration and upset of not being able to have any more children. I'd perhaps have more sympathy if Taylor had been childless, but she'd already given birth twice. Her plight was that she wanted children with her new partner, not that her maternal instincts were going haywire.

Taylor went on to organize a gender reveal party, during which friends and family joined to celebrate the baby and find out what the happy couple was having. They were expecting a girl - or rather, Reagan Simmons-Hancock was expecting a girl.

By this point, Taylor was wearing a fake baby bump. She even had professional pictures taken of her while she was "pregnant." Her boyfriend was none the wiser, although I find it difficult to understand how she was able to conceal this massive lie from him for months. She would have had to wear the bump almost all the time, intimacy must have been non-existent, and she must've been working overtime to keep on top of her plethora of lies. Did her boyfriend not want to attend the scans and checkups with her? Did Taylor put him off going or arrange them for when he was working? The answers to these questions remain unknown, but it's baffling to understand how the closest person to her wasn't able to sniff out any sort of deception.

All the while, she was gaining Reagan's trust, getting as close to the soon-to-be mother as she possibly could. Taylor was keeping an eye on her victim, ensuring she knew when the right time to pounce would be. In her plan, there would have to be a death; Taylor was well aware and prepared for this. As Reagan's due date was etching closer, Taylor decided October 9, 2020, was the date her wicked plan would come to fruition.

In anticipation of the new baby arriving, Taylor told her boyfriend she'd be getting induced that day and planned to meet him at the hospital. She was going to be there already, a newborn baby in her arms, acting upset that her partner had missed the birth of their first child. In reality, she intended to drive there after slicing the baby from Reagan.

The plan was set. Taylor headed to Reagan's home in New Boston, scalpel in her bag, ready to kill and abduct. What happened was more brutal than you could imagine.

Once inside the home, Taylor stabbed her victim more than 100 times, violently and rapidly piercing her body with jab after jab. The mother-to-be was in no shape to defend herself. She was heavily pregnant, exhausted from taking care of her toddler, and had no clue of the hidden malice her new friend had for her. Reagan cried out for help, lying on her floor and bleeding out quickly. Taylor retrieved the hammer she'd brought and battered the young mother's head with it. Reagan was badly injured from the frenzied attack but battled to stay alive and save her children. Her three-year-old toddler was close by, watching the sick attack taking place. It's what kept Reagan fighting. Then, the beaten mother felt pain like never before; Taylor Parker had sliced her open and was removing Braxlynn from her womb.

Reagan's toddler had to watch her mother die in front of her while the attacker fled with the baby.

Taylor kept the cord to make it seem like she'd just birthed the child and headed to a hospital an hour away. The baby had been in the womb for seven and a half months, meaning her premature "birth" was a high risk for complications. Not only that, the traumatic and disturbing way the baby had been ripped from her mother no doubt caused the child stress, so it's no surprise that the baby tragically passed away on the drive to the hospital. Still, Taylor assembled the cord to make it appear like she'd birthed the child. She was speeding her way to Oklahoma, which caught the attention of a passing police officer, who pulled her over.

The speeding woman had a newborn on her lap, the cord still tucked in her pants, and was frantically making her way to the hospital. This was an understandable reason for speeding; the officer agreed and got her to Oklahoma, where her twisted lies began to unravel. It was clear to medical professionals that this woman had not just given birth. But who had?

An hour away in New Boston, Reagan lay dead on the floor of her home. Her mother had gone around to visit her and stepped into a scene she will never be able to wipe from her memory. Her daughter, lying in an unbelievable amount of blood, her stomach ripped from hip to hip, with her baby no longer there. She called the police immediately, her heartbreak and grief only dampened by the three-year-old granddaughter who needed her more than ever.

There was no way out for Taylor, who'd now been cornered by the police at the hospital. She had to face up to the vile crime she'd carried out that brutally ended the life of a young mother and her baby. Not to forget the toddler who was stripped of her mother. News of the crime hit local headlines, with Taylor being called the "womb raider."

The prosecution's case was cut and dry. There wasn't much argument against Taylor's guilt, but her defense tried to minimize her role in the murder by explaining that the woman wasn't in her right mind when she carried out the shocking crimes. She was human, they argued, and nobody around her was helping her despite the wheels clearly coming off in front of them. At least some of her friends or family, the defense argued, ought to have known something was amiss with Taylor's "pregnancy." And still, nobody questioned her about the inaccuracies, the slip-ups, the strangeness of it all. She'd had a hysterectomy, after all. *Did they think she was a medical wonder?*

Taylor's defense did have one tough task on their hands, however. They fought to prove the baby was never alive, which would have dismissed the kidnapping charge against her. If they could get rid of the abduction charge, they could have gotten the death penalty sentence taken off the table. Their argument was the baby didn't have a heartbeat when Taylor took her, making it impossible to kidnap a human that wasn't alive. However, the prosecution brought in a number of medical experts who testified that little Braxlynn had a heartbeat when born.

The odds were stacked against Taylor, who wept throughout the trial. In October 2022, Taylor Parker was sentenced to death for the chilling crimes she had committed two years earlier. Of the over 2000 people on death row in the USA, 50 are women. Taylor is now among that number.

Final Thoughts

Thank you for reading *Unbelievable Crimes Volume Four*. As you know, especially if you've read volumes one through three, the aim is to cover lesser-known cases.

Hopefully, most of these crimes are new to you. I would be doing my readers a disservice by covering crimes that had flooded headlines or had numerous documentaries made about them. True crime followers tend to know many of these awful crimes already, so I wouldn't be shining any light on those stories for you if I wrote about them. Lesser-covered crimes and their victims deserve acknowledgment and to be remembered. These crimes need to be kept in mind in order to learn from them: the mistakes that were made that led to such a horrific event being able to occur. The red flags that were missed. The wickedness of the perpetrator also shouldn't be forgotten. More importantly, the victim and their plight, suffering, and senseless end need to be remembered, too.

When I write these books, I use a list of potential cases that I have on a spreadsheet. I add to this list when a crime I'd forgotten about suddenly reappears in my thoughts or when a friend tells me about a case I'd not heard of. I pull out my phone and add it to the list. The spreadsheet is pretty big - so there are definitely a few more books worth there - but it's in no particular order. I pick the stories purely based on what I think will make the book well-rounded in terms of cases: different areas, different cultures, and different genders affected by the crimes. However, completely unintentionally, this book contains five crimes committed by teenagers. As I was writing this volume, it didn't register that I was typing tale after tale about killer teens.

I look at my nieces and nephews, and the idea that a teenager - or 12-year-old in Sharon Carr's case - is capable of murder just blows my mind in a terrifying way. The intent behind the murder in each case was different, but the ability to take another human being's life remained just as prevalent.

Once again, I'd like to thank you for reading and to let you know I truly value your readership. True crime followers are nothing if not loyal, and I appreciate you taking time out to read my books. If you find the time to leave a review, that would be so helpful for me in writing future books, and I'd be extremely grateful. I hope you enjoyed this fourth installment of the series. If so, book five is due to be released shortly. It includes some truly shocking stories, a few of which were new to me prior to researching them. If the *Unbelievable Crime* series interests you, I hope to see you there!

Until next time,

Daniela

My newsletter sign-up link:

Danielaairlie.carrd.co[1]

---

1. http://danielaairlie.carrd.co